ReadyGEN

GRADE

Text Collection

4

PEARSON

Glenview, Illinois • Boston, Massachusetts • Chandler, Arizona • Hoboken, New Jersey

Cover: Huguette Pizzic

ISBN-13: 978-0-328-85283-3
ISBN-10:   0-328-85283-X
1 2 3 4 5 6 7 8 9 10 V003 19 18 17 16 15

4000253203

Table of Contents

Unit 3 Exploring Impact and Effect

Unit 4 Creating Innovative Solutions

QUAKE!

DISASTER IN SAN FRANCISCO, 1906

GAIL LANGER KARWOSKI

ILLUSTRATED BY ROBERT PAPP

DISASTER
BEFORE DAWN

Jacob pulled back the covers and sat on the edge of his bed to take off his shoes. The dog jumped up and curled into a ball at the foot of the bed. Sliding onto his pillow, Jacob poked his feet out of the blanket and let his toes snuggle against the dog's soft fur. Together they drifted into sleep.

The sound of whining woke him. The dog was standing on his bed, tensed as if to run. Propping himself on an elbow, Jacob listened. He thought he could hear another dog barking in the distance. The room was dark and still; his father and sister seemed to be sleeping soundly. Stroking the dog's back, Jacob felt its muscles gradually relax. Finally, it settled down and rested its head on Jacob's thigh. Trying not to disturb it, Jacob eased back onto his pillow.

No sooner had he dozed off than the dog woke him again. This time it was scratching furiously at the covers as though it was digging a hole in a pile of leaves.

"Shhh," Jacob said. He listened, trying to decide if the movement had awakened Sophie or Papa. His sister's even breathing told him that she was still asleep, but he couldn't tell about Papa. Jacob leaned close to the dog and patted its head. "Hush, fella," he whispered.

The dog sat down but kept whining.

"What's going on, Jacob?" Itzak asked in a low voice.

Jacob felt the dog's body begin to tremble.

"Nothing," Jacob said. "He's such a young dog, I guess he misses his mother." Silence. Jacob wished he hadn't said the word "mother." He tapped his thigh softly until the dog nosed his hand. He ran his fingers through the fur around the animal's neck.

Too tense to fall back to sleep, Jacob stared at the shadows on the ceiling. He wished he could think of something to say. Something that would comfort Papa and make him cheerful again. Something that would make their family whole again.

Jacob must have nodded off because he woke with a start. This time the dog was poking him with its damp nose. When Jacob moved, the dog barked. The sound was sharp and loud, like a bullet in the night.

"What's the matter with the doggy, Jacob?" Sophie asked. Her voice echoed against the dark walls.

"Nothing," Jacob began.

"Jacob, that stupid animal has kept me up all night," Itzak said. "I told you there's something wrong with him." Jacob heard the bed creak as his father sat up. "I'm going to put him outside. He's already woken Sophie up. All we need is for the neighbors to complain."

Sophie shot out of bed. "No, Papa! The doggy will get lost. How can he find his way home in the night? He'll be scared."

Jacob stroked the dog's ears while Itzak coaxed Sophie back into bed. "Dogs aren't afraid of the dark," his father told her in a soothing voice, "because they see with their noses. This little dog is probably not used to being shut up inside a closed building so he's nervous. He's used to being outdoors." Itzak patted Sophie's back. Finally she slipped her thumb into her mouth and closed her eyes.

Jacob eased out of bed. "I'll take the dog outside," he whispered. "I guess I should have walked him after supper." He began to slip on his clothes.

"Be careful, son," Itzak said. "It's almost morning, and wagons will already be on the street. The drivers can't see so well in the dark."

Jacob nodded. "Maybe I'll walk over to the Produce District and wait for Uncle Avi. I'll leave the dog with him." He waited, hoping his father would stop him.

But Itzak did not speak until Jacob opened the door. "It's for the best, son," he said. "You'll see."

Jacob picked up the dog and carried it down the steps. He wasn't sure what time it was, but he heard sounds coming from one or two apartments. Most of the men who lived in their boardinghouse were laborers. Jacob knew that some of them got up before dawn to go to work.

As he opened the outside door, the dog squirmed like a worm on a hook. Then it jumped out of his arms and scrambled onto the street. Jacob could barely keep up as the dog charged down Howard Street. At the corner it began to howl. Jacob squinted, trying to see what the animal was so agitated about. The streetlights were on, but he couldn't see anything unusual. He heard other dogs barking in the distance.

"Is that why you're so restless, fella?" Jacob said. "Because of all the barking?"

The dog cocked its head as Jacob spoke. Then it dropped its chest to the ground, rump in the air, and barked. Leaping up, it ran around Jacob and onto the street. Again Jacob trotted to catch up.

At the next corner, Jacob could hear horses whinnying. *All the animals are skittish*, he thought. *That's strange.* When he reached First Street, Jacob turned north, but the dog darted off in the direction of the waterfront. Jacob slapped his legs, crouched down, and whistled. Finally he coaxed the dog back to his side.

When they reached Market Street, Jacob picked up the dog and carried it in his arms for a few blocks. It was so fidgety—Jacob was afraid it might dash under the wheels of a wagon.

The sky lightened from charcoal to smoky gray, and the streetlights began to dim. As Jacob hurried toward the Produce District, the dog's squirming became frantic. It thrust its hind legs against Jacob's chest and leaped. When it hit the ground, it let out a loud, shrill yelp.

"What's wrong, fella?" Jacob said. "We're going to see Uncle Avi. Come on."

The dog ran a few yards toward the docks, then turned and barked again.

"Not down there, fella," Jacob said. "This way." He trotted up the hill toward the Produce District.

The dog stood, undecided.

Over his shoulder, Jacob coaxed, "Come on, fella. This way."

At last the dog padded to Jacob. Side by side, they ran the rest of the way to Washington Street.

✳

The Produce District was already alive with activity. Jacob saw horses tethered to wooden wagons standing along both sides of the street. Men in overalls were unloading crates and sacks. Jacob breathed in the earthy smells of soil and horseflesh. He passed a wagon heaped high with bulging bags of potatoes and onions. A merchant rushed toward him carrying a stack of egg cartons, and Jacob stepped aside to let the man pass.

As Jacob hurried toward the spot where his Uncle Avi always set up his cart, he started to feel dizzy. His stomach churned, and he thought he was going to be sick. Jacob wondered if Papa was right and the dog had been trembling because of a disease.

The ground started to sway. Bending his knees, Jacob tried to ride the movement. The street heaved and rolled, like the ocean during a storm. It was as though a giant sleeping below the cobblestones had suddenly decided to get up.

Buildings began weaving in and out, and the street pitched like an angry sea. Jacob took a step forward and fell. He heard a wagon overturn and crates thud to the ground. Raising himself on all fours, he tried to make sense of what was happening. *This is an earthquake*, he realized. *It'll be over in a few seconds.* Jacob remembered several earthquakes and how the ground had seemed to roll. Sometimes dishes had fallen off shelves. But in an instant, the quakes had been over.

The street continued to heave and roll. Jacob's ears filled with a roar as loud as thunder. In the gray light he saw the cobblestone street split down the middle. A ditch several feet across opened! As Jacob watched, the ditch yawned wide, thinned to a slit, and gaped apart again.

Bricks were raining all over the street, and the roar was deafening. *I've got to get under something!* Jacob thought. Holding his arms over his head, he rushed toward an open building. He stumbled, then forced himself upright. Something rammed against his legs, and Jacob saw the dog. He could see its mouth moving up and down, but he could not hear it barking. Jacob tried to make his way toward the building again, but the dog tripped him. Frantic, Jacob changed direction and ran toward the other side of the street. A great cracking noise came from behind him. He whirled in time to see the front wall of the building collapse in a heap. The air filled with clouds of dust.

All along the street buildings rattled and lurched. Chunks of masonry hit the ground and broke into pieces. Window glass shattered. The columns on a nearby building buckled and crashed. Carts overturned, littering the sides of the street, and frantic horses struggled to free themselves from their reins.

The dog jumped on Jacob's thigh, pushing him backwards against a collapsed wagon. A pair of horses stampeded through the street toward them. They dragged a broken cart, which lurched from side to side and slammed into piles of fallen bricks. Jacob could feel his heart pounding inside his chest as he squeezed himself against the side of the heavy wagon, hoping it would give him some protection. He reached for the dog and held its trembling body close to his chest. The crazed horses careened by, missing them by just a few feet.

The roaring drowned all other sounds. Crouching beside the wagon, holding tight to the dog, Jacob watched the cobblestones vibrate and buildings cave in. The ground shook with such violence that Jacob thought the world was coming to an end.

The crazed horses careened by, missing them by just a few feet.

AFTERSHOCK

Jacob sat up, startled by the quiet. After the deafening roar of the earthquake, the absence of sound was eerie. The silence around him was so complete, he could hear the pounding of his own heart. Then somewhere far off in the distance, a child began to wail.

Jacob stood up, wiggled his head from side to side, and flexed his arms and fingers. He didn't feel pain anywhere, so he decided that he wasn't injured. The dog looked up at him and wagged its tail, and Jacob bent down to brush the dust off its face and whiskers.

The air had a peculiar, bluish yellow tinge that made everything seem unreal. The Produce District lay in shambles. Piles of dusty rubble littered the street, and some buildings had completely collapsed. Others looked ragged where large chunks of wall had fallen away. Railings dangled off balconies, and the cobblestone street was twisted and pitted. Jacob felt like he'd stumbled into the middle of a nightmare.

Lots of people were on the street. Some fell right to work, righting carts and gathering spilled merchandise. But others wandered aimlessly. Jacob saw one man wearing a nightshirt and walking with a slight limp. He wore a shoe on one foot, but his other foot was bare. A gray-haired woman held a small dog wrapped in a blue shirt. Several people clasped blankets around their shoulders; others carried boxes.

A woman bumped into Jacob. Her hair hung in disarray, and her face was smudged with soot. She carried a baby on one hip, and a small child clutched her skirt. The woman stared straight ahead, but Jacob was sure she hadn't seen him. When she stumbled on a fallen brick, she didn't even look down. Her eyes seemed fixed on something far away.

Nearby Jacob saw two heavyset men pushing with their shoulders against the side of an overturned wagon, while a third tossed aside sacks of onions and pieces of wood. Moans came from under the wagon. At last the workers uncovered an old man wearing an apron. He struggled out, grasping his left arm with his right hand. His shirt sleeve was torn, and blood oozed from a nasty gash on his arm.

Everybody avoided the sides of the street, where debris had fallen in huge piles. Glancing at the buildings, Jacob wondered if any more were going to collapse. He too moved toward the center of the street.

The dog began to bark—a high, excited sound. Jacob followed the dog down the street and saw a horse stuck in a ditch in the street. Only the horse's head and neck were visible. The poor animal's eyes bulged, and a froth of saliva dripped from its mouth. Jacob hurried to help it, but four or five men had already reached its side.

"Would you look at this!" one of them announced. "Poor beast fell right into the crack. Must've gotten crushed. It's dead." The man shook his head in disbelief.

Another man knelt beside the horse and looked into the gap between the cobblestones. The man whistled. "Holy Moses! I guess the street just opened up and swallowed it." The speaker turned to the others and used his hands to demonstrate. "Like a great big jaw—the ground must've opened wide and then clamped shut—squeezin' the life right outta this animal!"

People crowded around to see the wonder, but Jacob backed away. He was beginning to feel sick. So much destruction and horror! He headed down the hill, glancing up frequently to be sure that nothing was going to topple down on him from a damaged building. At street level the air was murky with the dust of collapsed buildings, but above the ruins Jacob could see the morning sun glistening in a clear blue sky. *How can the weather be sunny today?*

Suddenly he felt a jolt. *Another earthquake?* He looked at the people around him. Their eyes were wild with fright. Screams pierced his ears as the ground lurched and began to roll. Jacob fell to his knees and covered his head with his arms. The dog cowered against him.

The aftershock was over in a few seconds, but it energized the street. All at once the dreamy mood of unreality shifted and the entire area came alive with activity. People poured out of buildings carrying children, bundles of clothing, cartons. One man rushed by with a birdcage. All around Jacob people hurried in every direction.

For a second Jacob lost sight of the dog in the crowd. "Here, fella!" he called frantically. When he heard a familiar bark behind him, he whipped around. The dog ran toward him and jumped up. Jacob buried his hands in the thick fur of the dog's neck.

"Where should we go, fella?"

Before the earthquake, Jacob had been heading for Avi's produce stand to return the dog. Now he hesitated. Should he walk back up the hill and search for his uncle? A feeling in the pit of his stomach urged him to keep walking downhill. More than anything else, he wanted to be home with his family. *Papa will be worried sick about me.* Then another thought hit him hard, like a punch. *Papa! What if Papa is hurt? Or Sophie . . .* Jacob began to run. *Please, God, make them safe.*

Jacob had to slow down to pick his way around the piles of bricks and boards clogging the streets. In places, he scrambled over mounds of debris that completely blocked his way. People stood talking and pointing at the buildings, and Jacob had to squeeze past them. He mumbled, "Pardon me. Excuse me, I need to get through here."

Policemen were blowing their whistles and screaming orders. Horse-drawn wagons clattered down the street, their drivers yelling, "Make way for the horses!" One man glared at Jacob and hollered, "Move over, kid!"

A wagon pulled to a stop in front of a large building. The driver jumped off and hustled up the steps and into an open doorway. Moments later a man emerged and helped a woman in a long dress climb aboard the wagon. Further down the street Jacob saw several men hoisting large trunks onto wagon beds.

On Market Street the cable car tracks jutted out of the ground like mangled springs. Jacob threaded through twisted metal to get across the street.

As he ran, Jacob passed a family pulling a child's wagon piled high with possessions. A little dark-haired girl followed her father, her thumb in her mouth and her face grimy. The girl's eyes met Jacob's. She seemed so small and frightened. A vivid picture of Sophie filled Jacob's mind. He picked up speed and bolted around the family, the dog at his heels.

When they reached the next corner, a policeman blew his whistle to stop them. The road was completely blocked by fallen bricks. Two other policemen were directing eight or nine men as they hauled the bricks off the street. Jacob saw a motorcar idling on the other side of the pile of rubble.

"Clear the way!" the policemen shouted at pedestrians. "We've got to get this car through."

Jacob backtracked and turned onto a side street. He paused to catch his breath. *Where am I?* He knew he'd been heading in the general direction of home, but he hadn't paid attention to landmarks. He decided he'd better stop running willy-nilly because he was beginning to tire. His mouth felt very dry. Hoping to spot something familiar, he scanned the fronts of nearby buildings. He was in one of those streets that always reminded him of a canyon, flanked with tall buildings on both sides. This street had to be part of the business district.

All of a sudden the dog came rushing at him, barking furiously. *Why is the dog running toward me?* Jacob wondered. He didn't even remember the dog leaving his side.

Then he looked beyond the dog, and he felt like he was falling off a cliff. There, only a block away, a full-grown steer was stampeding down the street!

"Look out, sonny!" a voice shouted.

A steer? Jacob stood rooted to the spot. *Why is this happening? Who's yelling?*

A stab of pain snatched Jacob from his stupor. Something was snapping at his fingers and pulling at his clothes. He heard growling and glanced down. The dog was nipping at his fingertips.

The steer was hurtling down the street right at him! Jacob wheeled around, leaped over a fallen chimney, and threw himself against the wall of a building. As if in a dream, he watched the dog scurry out from beneath the pounding hooves of the steer. Dazed, he watched another steer thunder by, then two more.

Jacob heard shots ring out. He looked in the direction of the noise and saw two men with guns chasing after the cattle. One of the men paused and took another shot at the stampeding beasts. A steer keeled over sideways and hit the cobblestones with a thump. Jacob slid down the wall of the building and sat in a heap, his head in his hands.

"You alright, son?" said a voice in Jacob's ear.

Jacob turned his head. A middle-aged man wearing a black overcoat and hat was kneeling beside him. He looked like a well-dressed businessman out for a stroll.

"That was something, wasn't it?" The man chuckled, shaking his head. "Never thought I'd see a herd of cattle stampeding through the business district."

Jacob just gawked, too stunned to reply. He felt as if a perfect stranger had strolled right into the middle of his private dream and started a casual conversation.

"Good thing you had that dog with you," the man said. "I kept hollering, but I couldn't get your attention. I believe you would've been a goner if you'd stayed in the street."

Jacob tried to concentrate on the man's words, but they all blurred together in his head.

"Those cattle must've broken loose during the quake," the man continued. "The drivers were probably bringing them over to the stockyards at Portrero before everything went haywire."

Jacob nodded, but he was not at all sure what the man was saying.

The man sat down on a step. "Here, sonny. I took the precaution of filling a jug with water before I left home. Looks like you could use a drink."

When the man held out the jug to Jacob, the dog whined.

Laughing, the man poured a little water into his palm. "Guess you earned a drink, too," he said.

Wagging its tail, the dog approached the man slowly and slurped the water from his hand.

The man patted the dog's head. "That's all I can do for you, pooch," he said. "Don't know when I'll get my hands on any more water." He held out the jug for Jacob.

Jacob took a swig of the water, then another. "Thanks," he said. "I don't know what I was thinking when I saw that steer coming at me. I couldn't move." He handed back the jug.

"Where's your family, son?"

"Don't know," Jacob replied. "I was in the Produce District when the quake hit. I left my father and sister in bed this morning. I was trying to get back home. We live in a house south of Market Street."

"One of those wooden boardinghouses?"

Jacob nodded.

The man frowned. "I saw some folks coming from that direction. They said those houses were in bad shape. Some of them collapsed into a pile of sticks when the quake shook them. They said fires have already started down there. All the gas mains were damaged by the quake, you know."

Jacob gaped at the man.

"Look here, sonny, I wouldn't worry too much. Your family is probably fine. Folks have a way of getting through a calamity," he said. "Especially in this city. Lord knows we've had our share of earthquakes. This morning's temblor sure was something, though, wasn't it?"

Jacob couldn't sit still any longer. Every muscle in his body tingled with fear. He pictured Sophie trapped in the rubble and Papa frantically digging to reach her. He imagined curtains of flame roaring across buildings.

"I appreciate the water, mister," he mumbled as he stood up. "I've got to hurry." He stood up, then grabbed the wall to steady himself.

"You sure you're all right?" asked the man.

Jacob nodded. "I'm fine. Thanks." He stumbled into the street, the dog trotting beside him. Several people were bending over the huge body of the dead steer, but Jacob didn't go back for a closer glance.

When his legs began to feel steady under him, Jacob picked up speed. As he ran, he pictured Sophie's eyes when she was scared—round and dark, like pools brimming with fear.

SOUTH OF MARKET

By the time Jacob reached his street, he was panting. The sooty air stung his eyes. With so much dust in the air, he couldn't be sure... but he thought he smelled wood burning.

Pausing to catch his breath, Jacob took a careful look at his neighborhood. The familiar rows of boardinghouses and colorful shops were almost unrecognizable. The sky peeked through gaps where walls once stood. Many buildings had completely collapsed, leaving piles of broken boards between ruined houses. Signs were hanging off storefronts, and merchandise was scattered on the street.

One boardinghouse caught Jacob's attention. Tilting sharply, the structure rested on two of its foundation corners, as if it had frozen in the act of tipping over. A nutty thought popped into Jacob's mind, and he said aloud, "That building looks like it's doing a dance step!" At the sound of his voice, the dog whined and jumped up on Jacob's leg.

"We're almost there, fella. Just a few blocks to go."

Lots of people were on the street and debris was strewn all over the ground, so Jacob had to make his way slowly. Here and there among the piles of boards he spotted a broken chair, a man's hat, a broom handle. The familiar objects reminded him that hundreds of families lived South of Market. He wondered where all those people would go now that their homes were destroyed.

Jacob and the dog passed a man dragging a heavy trunk bound with ropes. The trunk made a rumbling sound as it bumped down the street. Every few minutes its owner stopped, sat down on his trunk, and mopped his forehead with a handkerchief.

They ran past an entire family trudging single file down the center of the street, like a row of ducklings. Both parents teetered under a load of blankets, pans, and other household items. Five children followed, from tallest to shortest. The first was a girl with long ringlets who held a violin case and an umbrella looped over her arm. Her four brothers trailed behind her, each carrying a heap of clothes. The smallest child couldn't have been any older than four, but he clutched a bundle of linens as he hurried after his bigger brothers.

Jacob swerved around a young man pushing a baby carriage piled high with towels, books, and a lamp. Walking next to the carriage was a woman who carried a sleeping baby wrapped in a quilt. Several people pushed wheelbarrows filled to overflowing with clothes and cooking utensils.

Sightseers also wandered through the streets, stopping to chat and gawk at the damage. A large group of men and women posed for a photograph in front of one of the wrecked buildings.

Just ahead, Jacob noticed four men on top of a mound of rubble. They were straining to hoist massive wooden beams and heave them aside. Two of the men kneeled to look at something, and one cupped his hands over his mouth and began to yell.

Those men are searching for people trapped under there! Jacob realized. His hands felt icy as he forced his legs to move. "Come on, fella, we need to hurry!"

Jacob and the dog had to circle around a crowd of twenty or thirty spectators who were gathered on the street looking up at a four-story hotel. The front wall of the hotel had simply peeled off, leaving the rest of the building intact. Jacob could see inside every room on every floor. There were lamps sitting on tables, beds with sheets on them, dressers, and shiny mirrors. A painting of a mountain hung against the yellow wallpaper in one room. It was like looking into a life-sized dollhouse.

The cutaway hotel made Jacob remember an afternoon last December. The weather had been mild, so he'd taken Sophie downtown to see the holiday decorations. It was just before Mamma died.

As they gazed in shop windows, Jacob had held his sister's hand. Sophie was fascinated by a fancy dollhouse in one window. He remembered how she had pointed out each miniature object. "Look, Jacob! See the tiny candleholder? It has a real candle in it. And there's a teeny tea set with roses on it!"

Jacob looked down and saw the dog watching him, its head cocked to one side.

"It's all right, fella," Jacob said. "We're gonna find them, you'll see."

When they reached the corner, Jacob had to glance up and down in each direction to be sure he knew where he was. Everything looked so different! The huge Nevada Boarding house had fallen in, leaving a mountain of rubble. Holding his breath, Jacob stared at the space next door. That's when he realized the impossible had happened. *Our house is gone!*

"Nooooo!" Jacob wailed as he charged into the jumble of boards and dust that had been home. "Papa! Are you here? It's me—Jacob! Answer me!"

The dog began barking and people were yelling, but Jacob ignored them. *Where's our apartment?* He had to find his family. He had to find Sophie!

As he scrambled onto the mound of boards, Jacob heard something crack. His foot plunged between some dusty planks, but he was able to break his fall by grabbing onto the corner of a mattress. Pulling his leg free, he continued crawling up the mound. Cautiously he inched across a jagged section of wall and squinted into a cavernlike opening. "Sophie! Papa! Can you hear me?" No voices answered, so Jacob picked his way around the opening and continued searching.

The dog was following him. Barking excitedly, it hopped from board to board. Suddenly it yelped, then began squealing frantically. Jacob looked back, but he couldn't see the animal. He heard claws scrabbling below him, so he kneeled to peer into the darkness beneath the boards. He could see the dog crouching near something that looked like a broken table.

Jacob shoved aside sticks and pipes and lowered himself into the pocket. The debris shifted and caved in around him. He grabbed at a massive headboard to slow his downward slide. Crawling toward the dog, he called, "Here I am, fella, I'm coming."

By stretching out his arm, Jacob could just reach the animal. It was clawing at the rubble with its front paws, but one of its hind legs seemed to be caught under something.

Jacob edged closer. Grasping the dog's body with one hand, he groped around with his other hand until he located its trapped leg. Then he tore away rough pieces of metal and splinters of wood. Carefully he dug around the leg until the dog was finally able to pull it out. As soon as he was free, the terrified animal leapt onto Jacob and knocked him off balance. Jacob barely managed to break his fall by grabbing the edge of a windowsill. He felt a stab of pain in his wrist, but he ignored it.

Clutching the squirming dog as tightly as he could, he edged backwards through the tangle. At last, half crawling, half staggering, he emerged from the pocket. When they were under the open sky again, the dog nestled close to Jacob's chest and licked his chin.

"Hey, kid!" a voice hollered from the street. "Whadda ya think yer doin'? Get offa there before ya break yer neck!"

A man scrambled partway up the mound and held out his arms. Jacob handed him the dog. "My family..." Jacob said hoarsely. "I'm trying to find them. We live in this building."

"Nobody's in this heap, kid. I been crawlin' around these buildings all mornin' lookin' fer folks who might've got trapped. Ain't heard a peep from this one." The man set the dog down near the street and grabbed Jacob's arm to help him scramble off the pile of debris.

"But my family...we live here..." Jacob tried to explain. "They were still in bed when I left...."

"Everybody got outta this house before the walls gave way. Least, everybody who was able to get out."

Jacob studied the man's face.

The man met Jacob's eyes. "Look, kid. There ain't no point in breakin' yer neck tryin' to dig through all this," the man said. "If yer family was trapped in this here building, they're goners, and that's the truth of it. If somebody was still alive here, we would've heard 'em screamin' by now. Lord knows we've heard plenty of screamin' next door, where the Nevada was!"

Jacob hesitated.

"Instead of breakin' yer neck up there, why don'tcha go ask around the street? Maybe somebody's seen yer folks."

Jacob scanned the jumble of boards, railing posts, furniture, and unidentifiable objects that was once their boardinghouse. He really didn't know where to begin tunneling to uncover their apartment, and it was plain that he couldn't sort through this entire mound by himself. The man's suggestion made sense. Maybe somebody on the street had seen Papa and Sophie.

Brushing little nuggets of broken glass off his sleeve, Jacob noticed his wrist was bleeding. But he ignored the trickle of blood and said, "Maybe you know my father? He's pretty tall and thin, with dark hair. Itzak Kaufman's his name. He's a butcher. He would have had a little girl with him—my sister Sophie. She's five. Curly hair and big brown eyes."

The man shrugged. "Sorry, kid. I don't know the name. And yer describin' hundreds of folks down this way."

Jacob nodded, stamping his feet to shake off some of the dust.

The man ripped a length of fabric off the hem of his shirt and motioned for Jacob to hold out his bleeding arm. "I don't see any shards of glass in here," he said as he tied the fabric around the wound. "Better wash it clean when ya get a chance, though."

Jacob sniffed. "Do you smell something burning?" he asked.

The man frowned. "Fire's comin' this way. It's three, maybe four streets over. Fires are startin' all over the city. And with the water lines cracked, ain't no way to put 'em out. Don't know what we're gonna do—" He shook his head. "Even if the city had enough fire engines to go around, how could them wagons get through the mess in the streets? Guess it don't matter down here, though.

Who's gonna worry about these cheap boardinghouses, with them big fancy buildings downtown in danger of burnin' up?"

"Hey, Mac!" a voice called from the collapsed Nevada House.

"Over here!" yelled the man who was helping Jacob.

"Think I got somebody. Can you give a hand?"

Jacob followed Mac, who hurried back to the mountain of debris where the Nevada Boarding House once stood.

"Better stay back, kid," said Mac. "Don't want ya gettin' hurt again." He disappeared into what looked like a tunnel leading down into the ground. It was dark at the bottom, and Jacob could see water seeping through the boards. After a few moments Mac and three other men emerged from the hole, balancing the body of a woman on a long board. Jacob helped clear a path for them to the street.

A knot of onlookers crowded around the men, pushing in to see the body as the men laid it down. Jacob looked at their faces and understood that these people were searching for their families, too. When the rescuers carried out a lifeless body, all the people waiting on the street hurried over, praying the dead person wasn't somebody they knew and loved.

Jacob edged into the group. Two of the rescuers were standing with their heads bowed in prayer. Eyes closed, they held their right hands over their hearts. He heard someone wailing. The dog pushed through Jacob's legs and sat on his foot. Jacob bent down and picked him up.

One large man broke away from the group. Mac grabbed the man's arm and said, "Hold on, Callahan. Surely you can spare a minute for a bit of a prayer. This is Duncan O'Connor's mum."

Jacob gasped. *Timothy's grandmother! That's the woman I met last night. I offered to carry her bundles up the stairs for her.*

He stared at the body. Mrs. O'Connor looked so different that he barely recognized her. She was as motionless as a fallen tree, but her eyes were wide open. A long nightshirt clung to her white body, and the skin on her bare legs glistened with moisture. Her gray hair was pasted against her head and her face was puffy. The skin on one side of her forehead was bruised and purple, like something had fallen on her while she was lying in bed.

Forcing himself to shut his eyes, Jacob tried to remember the words of the Kaddish, the Hebrew prayer for the dead that he'd recited so often after his mother's death. But his heart was thumping so fast that he couldn't think. Icy prickles of terror ran up and down the skin on his arms.

Fear washed over Jacob

A little girl tugged at the skirt of the woman next to Jacob. "Why is she all wet, Mamma?"

"I dunno. Maybe the water line broke and flooded the bottom floors."

"But where's Timothy? Didn't he live with his granny?" the child asked. "Is Timothy all right?"

"I dunno, child. I haven't seen Timothy, but he might've gotten out earlier. Don't keep pesterin' me with so many questions right now. They been carryin' folks outta there all mornin', and it looks like anybody left in there's been drowned."

Fear washed over Jacob. *What about Papa and Sophie? Please God, don't let them be drowned.*

He backed away from the cluster of people and stumbled into the street, the dog following at his heels. Jacob's stomach was queasy, and his arms and legs felt shaky. He flopped onto the ground and closed his eyes.

The dog nosed Jacob's neck. When Jacob didn't move, the dog whined and licked the boy's nose with its sticky tongue. Jacob sat up and opened his eyes, grimacing at the sour odor of the dog's breath. He stroked the animal's ears while he peered around the street. Lots of people were standing in little clumps on the street, but he didn't see anybody he knew. *I guess most of our neighbors have already left,* he thought. *Where did everybody go?*

Leather shoes were scattered around the street near where he sat. Jacob reached for one. Its heel was missing. *This must be from Mr. Straussberg's shop.* Jacob wondered if the old cobbler, who lived in a room behind his shop, had made it out in time.

Picking himself up, Jacob brushed off the seat of his pants. He took a deep breath and walked over to a man leaning on a wheelbarrow full of clothing. "Pardon me," he said. "My name's Jacob. Jacob Kaufman. We live in that house next door to the Nevada. Have you seen my father—Itzak Kaufman, the butcher? He's got dark hair. He'd have my sister with him. She's only five—dark curly hair."

The man shook his head.

Jacob thanked him and went from person to person, asking the same questions. They all tried to be helpful, but nobody knew Itzak Kaufman. Nobody remembered seeing a man and a girl that matched their description.

"Sorry, son," a tall woman told him. She had tears in her eyes. "I can't find my father, either. He's so crippled up with the rheumatiz that he can hardly walk. I've been searching for him all morning."

"A lot of families got separated," another woman muttered.

"Try not to worry, kid—you'll find 'em."

Finally a freckled woman with a kerchief tied around her hair smiled at Jacob. "I think I know who you're talking about," she said. "Your father's the butcher, isn't he?"

"Yes," Jacob said. He held his breath.

"I used to buy meat from him," she continued. "His wife died not too long ago, right?"

Jacob nodded. "Have you seen him?"

"I saw someone who looked like him on the street this morning. Maybe an hour or two ago. He was carrying a little girl. She had her thumb in her mouth."

"That's her!" Jacob said. "That's Sophie."

They're alive! Both of them. Jacob felt like flying. "Do you know where they went?"

The woman shook her head. "No, can't say I do. But maybe somebody else saw them." She turned and called to a red haired man in a cap. "Eddie! You remember the butcher, Mr. Kaufman? He lived in the same building as Fritz. Have you seen him? This is his son."

The man nodded at Jacob. "Kaufman the butcher? Yes, I know your da. Saw him this mornin', I did. Right after the big shake." He looked around the street. "But that was a couple of hours ago. Don't know where he is now. Maybe you got an aunt or granny livin' down here?"

"No, my uncle—" Suddenly a thought flashed through Jacob's mind. "I know where they went! Papa thinks I'm at Uncle Avi's stand. He must've gone looking for me there!" Jacob exclaimed. He shook the man's hand up and down. "Thank you, mister. Thank you." Tears slid down Jacob's cheeks. He wiped them with his sleeves and stammered, "See, I was afraid that..."

"Of course you were!" The man patted Jacob's shoulder. "I understand," he said. "It's only natural. You were afraid your da got crushed when the building fell. That's how any man would feel."

Swallowing hard, Jacob tried to steady his voice. "Well, I'll be seeing you," he said. "Good luck, and thanks again for your help."

Jacob took off at a trot, heading back toward Market Street. The dog bounded along beside him.

EARTHSHAKER'S BAD DAY

by Gaby Triana

Long ago, the great god Poseidon, ruler of the seas, horses, and earthquakes, sat on his golden throne in his glorious and sparkling palace at the bottom of the deep Aegean Sea. Surrounded by gleaming gems, pearls, and coral of every color, Poseidon scratched his beard, held his trident, and thought about his life. Here he was, living in the most beautiful palace in all of the world, and yet still he was unhappy.

As one of the twelve gods of Mount Olympus, Poseidon was powerful. After all, his brothers were Zeus, god of the sky, and Hades, god of the underworld. He could have anything he wanted. So *why* then, did he always feel so lonely?

He knew what the people on land were up to, as gods usually did. He heard they had built a new city, not far away, in a land called Attica. He'd heard that King Cecrops, half-human and half-snake, was looking for a patron god for his new city. *Maybe I could be their god?* If the king chose him, then he could be near humans *all* the time, instead of alone in the sea. Maybe they would even name the city after him!

But two things were against him. What if the people on land didn't *want* the great god of the seas to be their patron? And second, his niece Athena also wanted to rule over the city. Athena was not only the goddess of wisdom, she was also Zeus's daughter. Everybody loved her. She and Poseidon argued over who would head the new city for countless weeks.

Poseidon pouted on his throne more and more.

What could he do to show the people that he was the right choice? Once, long ago, he created horses as a gift to people. He wanted to give humans a strong animal to help them carry heavy loads and transport them wherever they needed. *It was such a caring creation,* he thought. Yet the other gods frowned upon him.

"You are causing problems with these horses!" Zeus bellowed at him. "The people who have them think they are better than the people without! Wars are starting because of you!"

Poseidon felt terrible about causing such strife. He had only wanted to help.

His sadness made the clouds darken. The waves churned gray and frothy. To clear his mind, Poseidon called for his golden chariot and team of six snow-white horses. Maybe a quick dash across the ocean would help him feel better. He leaped in and held the reins tightly. As the chariot bounced across the choppy waters, Poseidon spotted someone swooping down from the sky toward him in the distance.

A moment later, a young man arrived wearing winged shoes. "King Poseidon," the young man said, hovering in the air. He held a staff decorated with snakes and wings.

"Nice to see you again, Hermes," Poseidon said flatly.

"Sir, King Cecrops summons you for a contest."

"A contest?" Poseidon's sea blue eyes sparkled. He loved to show off.

"Yes. Against your niece, Athena. Come to the Acropolis in Attica at once." Then, Hermes took off, soaring westward over the sea.

Poseidon knew the location of this city. It sat on a large hill known as the Acropolis and it was the perfect place to hold a contest. He would go at once and find out what this competition was all about.

As Poseidon's mood improved, the clouds opened. The sun shone again. The waves parted to allow his horses through. When he arrived at the Acropolis, he was surprised to see the entire city gathered at the foot of the flat-topped hill. In the sky, ten of his fellow Olympian gods, including Zeus and Hades, sat smiling down at everyone. Standing regally on the hill was Athena, beautiful daughter of Zeus, dressed in silk robes, wearing a gleaming helmet, and holding her staff.

"Hello, Uncle," she said.

"Athena." He nodded at her.

"Welcome, both of you." King Cecrops slithered up the Acropolis towards them. "The people of Attica are unsure of whom to pick as their new patron god. Shall we have a contest to help us decide?"

Poseidon looked at Athena. She was beautiful, wise, and patient, but his powers were also great. He knew he could win this contest. He was the mighty ruler of all the seas! "Yes, let us compete," Poseidon said.

Athena bowed her head at him with a smile.

"Good," King Cecrops said. "Then let each of you design a gift for these fine people. Whoever gives the best gift wins the city."

Poseidon thought for a moment. *A gift? That's all?*

The people built their city near the sea because they loved water. *Perfect.* Even though he was known as the Earthshaker in some parts of the land for causing earthquakes when angry, ruling the sea was what he did best. Slowly, he lifted his trident, brought it down with force, and struck a large rock. Right away, a large spring full of water formed, and the people cheered.

"With this water, you may drink and bathe," he said, but when the people rushed over to drink the water, they spit it back onto the ground.

"It is too salty!" they cried.

Being a sea god, salty water was all Poseidon could create. He raised a hand and explained, "Yes, but it represents the sea and important trade with other lands. You will have a big empire of ships. Our city will be the greatest in all the land!"

The people liked the idea of having a spring to symbolize their greatness, but they also wanted to see what gift Athena might give them.

Athena stepped forward, looked at the surrounding land, and smiled. Using her staff, she pointed the end at the ground. With a flash of light, a beautiful tree rose from the ground. "Behold the olive tree," she told the people. "It can give you food, oil, wood, and shade. It can also be a great product for trade."

The people cheered and clapped for the gift Athena had created for them.

"That is silly," Poseidon said, jealous. "It's just a tree."

"And yours is just a pool of salty water, Uncle." Athena laughed. "My gift is wiser and more practical. Isn't it, Father?" She looked up at Zeus in the heavens. He beamed down at her, thunderbolt in hand.

"Tell us, dear gods, which gift do you find better for my fine people?" King Cecrops asked the other nine Olympians. Zeus did not vote. He wanted to stay fair, since both his brother and daughter were competing for the same prize.

The other Olympians talked amongst themselves. Soon, it was decided. Athena had created the better gift, so she would become the patron ruler! She bowed to thank everyone. The people named their city Athens after their goddess of wisdom.

As the townsfolk cheered and celebrated, Poseidon shook with rage. His voice boomed across the sky, and the clouds darkened. The winds blew stronger. "Water is the source of all life!" he shouted. "You chose a silly tree over a symbol of true strength and might! You will all be sorry!"

And with that warning, he jumped back into his chariot and raced across the land toward the crashing sea. *Why don't humans ever appreciate my gifts?* he wondered. His offerings were just as wise and practical as Athena's. Thunder and lightning crackled over the ocean, as Poseidon fought to control his anger. Not only had he lost the contest, but he had lost to his brother's daughter.

Embarrassed, Poseidon plunged deep underwater, fuming in anger. He lifted his trident, gave it a mighty whirl, and brought it down with all his power onto the bottom of the ocean floor. When it struck, a giant crack appeared. The ocean floor trembled. A giant wave rose to the surface. He struck the ground again, making the earth rumble and quake. The earthquake created a giant, rippling wave that traveled quickly in all directions. One of the waves raced toward Attica, where the people of Athens were still celebrating the outcome of the contest.

The tidal wave reached the shore and spilled onto the land. It spread everywhere, reaching Athens and all of northern Attica. People fled in all directions. Most of them gathered on the Acropolis to wait for the floodwaters to go down and for the ground to stop shaking.

When Poseidon calmed down, the skies returned to their normal blue. The ocean once again flattened. After a while, the floodwaters in Attica went down. The people were able to go on living and worshipping Athena as their chosen god.

Later on, Poseidon returned to visit Athens. He discovered that everyone still worshipped him. They built a temple on the Acropolis called the Parthenon. On the temple were scenes of him and Athena creating their gifts. The spring he created was still there as a deep well. Poseidon felt terrible about having lost his temper, but he also learned he could still be important to the people without being their patron god.

While he and Athena continued to fight for many more years, they sometimes worked together to protect the city. And every time the people of Athens felt the ground rumble and shake beneath their feet, they knew it was just Poseidon, the Earthshaker, having a bad day.

The Monster Beneath the Sea

by Stacia Deutsch

Deep in the ocean, off the coast of Japan, lived a catfish named Namazu. Like all catfish, Namazu didn't need to use his small eyes to find his way through the salty waters. He used his cat-like whiskers to sense the sea around him. With a flick of his tail, he was propelled whichever way he wanted to go.

But Namazu was different from the other catfish of the Pacific Ocean in one important way. He was enormous; a monster-sized fish that lived alone in a rocky lair along the ocean floor. Namazu was so large that even the smallest flick of his tail caused giant waves to crash on the shore above and stirred earthquakes throughout the island nation of Japan.

When Namazu wiggled, even just a tiny bit, the buildings in Japan rattled. Glass windows shattered. Shelves collapsed, scattering merchants' goods across floors. Tea spilled. The very earth groaned and cracked. The people knew how to duck their heads and run for shelter.

No one was safe when Namazu shook his massive tail.

One day, a young artist was at his worktable using a sharp chisel to create a woodcut. He'd spent months crafting a detailed representation of the capital city of Edo where he lived. Painstakingly, he etched out shapes and lines of shops, buildings, streets, and miniature people in an intricate design. The woodcut was nearly finished, ready to be covered with ink and pressed against a sheet of parchment. Very carefully, he set his knife against the block for the final stroke, when far below the sea, Namazu decided it was time to stretch out and move around.

The giant catfish inched along the deep, dark surface of the sea. Using his whiskers, he smelled and tasted the sea. He moved past a school of tuna and through a seaweed garden. Then, near a long, rocky coral reef, Namazu raised his tail and smacked it against the ocean floor.

Sand splattered.

A whirl of water bubbled from the impact.

With a boom and a bang, the crust of the earth crumbled.

A crack expanded out from the place Namazu's tail slapped down and continued along the sea floor. Energy under the earth's crust built up until it was dangerously stressed, and then it exploded. The entire island of Japan shook violently as the ground quaked.

The earthquake knocked over the artist's worktable, toppling his tools to the ground. The chisel he'd been using to carve a tiny pagoda slipped, leaving a deep jagged scratch across the small square of wood.

The artist looked at his wood block. It was ruined.

Tears filled his eyes. This was not the first time a swish of Namazu's tail had caused a quake that destroyed his work. Broken bits of block littered the workshop floor. The artist closed his eyes and sighed. He did not want to start over again.

In that moment, he decided to quit and give up his dream of becoming an accomplished artist who would have his work displayed in every home and shop throughout Japan. He would look for a more practical job, one that would not be affected by Namazu's many quakes. Perhaps he should become a bricklayer, repairing the buildings that were constantly toppling down.

As the artist began to pack his tools into a canvas bag, he heard commotion outside on the street. He left his studio to discover that people were gathering in the town's central square.

"We must do something about Namazu," the baker said. His jacket was covered with spilled rice flour dust and splattered with frosting.

"I agree." A woman came from the tea ceremony house, carrying pieces of an ornate broken kettle and shards of ruined teacups.

Behind her, parents, children, bankers, chefs, and merchants gathered. The entire town was uniting for an important meeting.

"This has gone on too long," the baker said, standing before the assembly. "We must call upon Kashima to help us."

A hush settled over the crowd. No one made a sound.

"Kashima is too busy to handle this matter," a woman said, as she cradled a small baby in her arms. "He is the god of martial arts and must oversee the dojos." Dojos were the training centers for students learning karate, judo, and samurai.

"He is the sword god and must visit his shrines," someone else added.

The baker said, "Kashima is the only god who can protect us from Namazu."

After a long moment, the artist stepped forward. He set down his bag of tools. "I will go. I will ask Kashima for help."

The artist heard people talking about his bravery as he left the square, but he didn't feel very brave. He was only doing what he felt was necessary. And he was scared.

The artist went to the dojo to find Kashima. The god was in the shrine, listening to prayers and accepting offerings. There was a long line that wrapped around the building. The artist stood in the back and waited his turn. As he moved closer to where the god sat, his knees began to shake. A bead of nervous sweat formed on the artist's forehead. He had never spoken to a god directly before and did not know what to expect. Would the god listen to his request and offer assistance? Or would the god laugh and send him away in shame?

A woman left the dojo crying. A man walked by smiling. A child came out of the shrine carrying a bag of gold coins. A young couple emerged, arms wrapped happily around each other.

When the artist reached the front of the line, he was terrified to be in such a mighty presence. His words felt thick in his throat as he explained about Namazu and the earthquakes.

Kashima immediately understood the importance of the artist's plea. He announced, "I will go and speak to Namazu."

Grateful and filled with hope, the artist accompanied the god to the seashore and sat down on a decaying dock. He would wait there until Kashima returned.

Kashima descended under the sea and found Namazu resting in his lair.

"I have come on behalf of the people of Japan," Kashima told the fish. "The earthquakes are destroying their towns. Buildings are unsafe. People are getting hurt."

"It would be against my nature as a fish not to shake my tail," Namazu said.

"You can choose to control yourself," Kashima said. "You must avoid hitting the bottom of the sea. Stop making trouble for the island!"

"No." Namazu laughed. "I won't. I like to smack my tail on the bottom of the sea. I like it when the earth shakes."

"You are putting the island in danger." He raised a sword and demanded, "No more earthquakes."

The fish replied with a laugh.

Kashima pinned Namazu's tail to the ground with two long blades.

The fish gave a mighty roar and, with a great thrust of his body, broke free.

"You cannot stop me," Namazu declared. "Watch this, Kashima. I can make small tremors—" He wiggled his tail and the land above shivered. "Or large quakes that will destroy entire cities." Namazu raised his tail, ready to show Kashima his power and destructive force.

Kashima looked quickly around. Swords were a mighty weapon, but not solid enough to hold the monster fish. He needed something bigger, stronger, and heavier. Near the lair, Kashima found what he needed. "I have promised to help the people of Japan," Kashima told Namazu.

With a mighty roar, Kashima leapt on the great catfish's back. It was well known that Kashima was not only the sword god and the god of martial arts, but he was also an expert at sumo, the Japanese sport of wrestling. The god and fish wrestled, rolling over and over, creating a storm of sand along the ocean floor and a torrent of waves up above.

"There will always be earthquakes!" the fish declared.

"Not while I am here." Raising a giant rock off the ocean floor, Kashima thrust the rock onto Namazu's back. With all his might, the catfish tried to get out from under the stone, but he could not free himself. Exhausted, Namazu lowered his tail in defeat. He was trapped, unable to create the smallest earthquake or even a tiny water wave.

With Namazu safely imprisoned, Kashima rose to the surface of the water and met the young artist at the shore.

"It is done," Kashima announced.

"Thank you," the artist said. He gave the god an offering of fruit and flowers. The people of Edo came to the dock to sing Kashima's praises.

"I will stay below the ocean and make sure that Namazu doesn't break free," Kashima told the people. "But I cannot watch him every minute of every day. There are times I must visit my shrines and accept my offerings." Kashima tilted his head toward a fishing boat that floated in the harbor. "When I am gone, Ebisu, the god of the fishermen, will protect the city."

"Ebisu is known to fall asleep on the job," the young artist reminded the god in a whisper.

"True. It has happened before. . . ." Kashima considered the problem. He looked out to sea, toward the spot where Namazu was

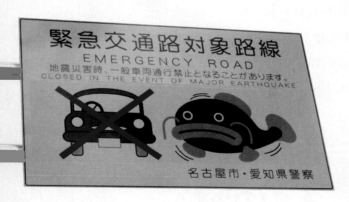

secured under the rock. To the artist, he said, "You must create an earthquake warning system. Design an image of Namazu and tell people to place it on road signs throughout Japan. It's important that the people know what to do if Namazu swishes his tail."

"I will begin the artwork right away," the young artist assured Kashima with a quick bow.

Kashima bowed low to the men and women of Edo, then turned and disappeared into the sea.

ESCAPE FROM POMPEII

CHRISTINA BALIT

On a hillside overlooking the sparkling Bay of Naples, the Roman city of Pompeii glimmered in the sunlight.

From his window, young Tranio listened to the noise humming from bars, taverns, and shops around him, and to the busy tradesmen haggling in the streets below. Beyond the massive city walls he could see Pompeii's greatest protector looming in the distance. They called it Vesuvius, the Gentle Mountain.

Could anyplace feel safer than here, Tranio wondered? Was anything more beautiful?

Tranio was the son of Dion the actor and lived with his parents near the Theater District of Pompeii. He'd often sneak to the harbor at the mouth of the River Sarnus and hide behind sacks of grain. There he'd watch pots of wine, oil, and spices being carried to and from the ships, or fishermen unloading their rich catches.

ROCVLA

Sometimes Tranio went to the forum to listen to the politicians make their speeches, the shopkeepers argue, and the poets sing.

His favorite song was:

Rumble down, tumble down,
 great city walls,
Feel the ground grumble,
 the citizens stumble
When the earth shakes, and
 rumble down, tumble down.

Everyone would join in, laughing as they remembered the earthquake tremors. A few years before Tranio was born, there had been a big earthquake in Pompeii, and parts of the town had still not been fully repaired. But nobody took tremors seriously anymore.

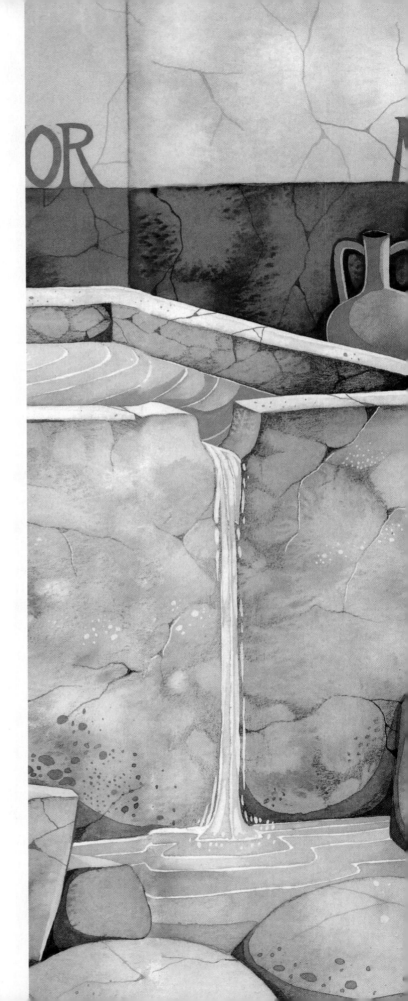

On other days, Tranio would shout up to Livia, the baker's daughter, who lived across the street, "Liv! Stop curling your hair and come and play jacks! I've got a bag of bones from my mother's kitchen! They're just the right size!"

Livia spent most of her time learning to weave and cook, but during the hot afternoons she and Tranio would sit by the fountain and play knucklebones, or chase dogs down the street.

One hot August day, Dion took Tranio through a shady passage into one of Pompeii's two theaters on the edge of the city, where a pantomime was being rehearsed.

"Sit on the steps, son, and learn!" said Dion. "We'll be using you in small parts soon."

To begin with, Tranio enjoyed watching the sword fights and strutting clowns. The masked actors playing thieves and devils and the leaping acrobats quite took his breath away. But eventually his attention began to wander….

hen something happened . . . The stone steps creaked, the boards began to rattle, and the building quivered. Props fell to the stage and scenery split. Tranio's father froze to the spot. Everyone was silent.

But one by one the actors began to relax. "Rumble down, tumble down, here we go again!" they chanted.

"Nothing to fear, everybody!" called Tranio's father. "Back to rehearsal, please." The actors fastened their masks and carried on as if nothing had happened.

But Tranio wriggled through the curtain and ran down the street.

He ran as fast as he could to Livia's house. Everyone was shouting, arguing, carrying belongings outside to safety.

"Livia!" he called. "Liv, where are you?" The bakery was empty. Loaves lay scattered on the floor, the oven blazed, and the small donkey turning the grain mill brayed and jumped nervously against its chain.

"Tranio!" Livia leapt down the stairs. "Father's chasing our goat through the market! The poor old thing bolted when the ground began to grumble. You'd have died laughing. Come on!"

Flushed and excited, the two children ran hand in hand into the dusty streets.

But as they ran, the sky began to darken and a thick cloud drifted slowly overhead.

Livia turned to Tranio. "Why are the seagulls flying toward the woods? They're going the wrong way."

A small bird in a hanging cage chirped frantically, trapped behind its bars as the air began to fill with ash.

Livia coughed. "Tranio . . . perhaps we should go back."

Tranio grabbed her hand. "We can't go back. The dust is too thick. Quick—the harbor! Run! Just run!"

Boats were bobbing on the choppy water as men began to untie lines from their moorings. No one noticed two small children climb up the narrow plank of a small Greek cargo ship and hide beneath a pile of colored rugs. Dusty and tired in their hiding place, they soon fell asleep.

But as they slept, the anxious captain untied his boat. He sensed that the winds had changed direction and that the air was uncomfortably hot. The sea began to churn and pull back from the shore.

When Tranio and Livia woke and looked out, they were horrified. Pompeii was getting farther and farther away. The sky was now thick with pumice and black with ash.

"Tranio, I can't breathe . . . in the back of my throat . . . ." As she spoke, Livia started to choke. The children could hear dogs barking and people's muffled screams as they ran gasping for air with rags covering their mouths or pillows over their heads. Some people fell to the grumbling, trembling ground.

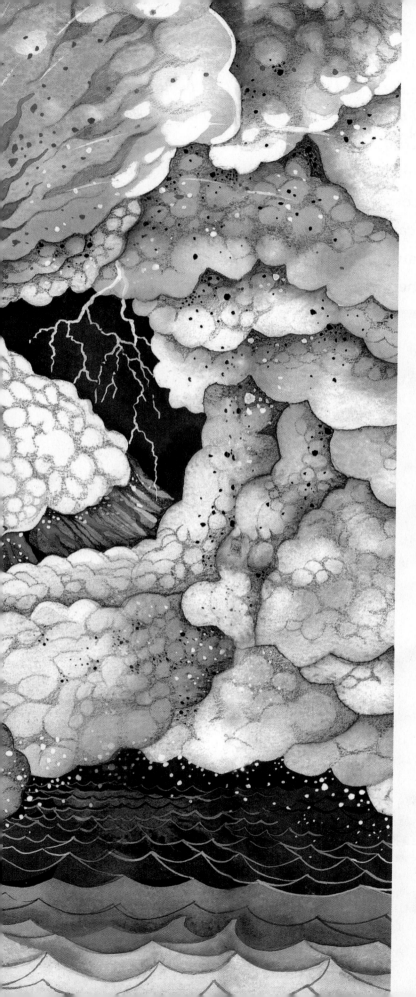

And then, in one terrible endless moment, they heard mighty Mount Vesuvius roar. Its top exploded in a scream, and flames ripped upward to the sky. A massive cloud of silver ash rose to the heavens, twisting and bubbling in all directions, until everything was in total darkness.

Lightning flashed and thunder roared. Streams of molten liquid flowed in fast rivers down the mountain slopes and covered a nearby town. The walls, streets, and gardens of their beloved Pompeii disappeared beneath a blanket of ash and stones. Before their very eyes, everything and everyone they had ever loved were destroyed.

Tranio and Livia held each other desperately when the steaming lava reached the sea itself. The water began to swell against the sides of the boat as it moved slowly out to safety.

They had left just in time. Soon the sea sank back from the shore and even the fish were stranded there.

*M*any years passed . . . and the mountain grew cool and still. At first its slopes were burnt and barren, but in time plants began to grow as the volcanic soil brought forth its riches once more. Most people had forgotten the buried city.

An old man and woman stood in the shade of an orange tree and laid flowers there. Long ago, they had been rescued by the kind captain of a Greek cargo ship, and he had raised them as his own. They were Tranio and Livia, saying farewell to those buried under the ash beneath their feet.

"We won't forget you," they whispered.

Would anyone ever find their beloved Pompeii? they wondered. Would anyone ever see its splendid streets? Perhaps. Perhaps not.

Tranio and Livia walked back to their small house beside the orange grove. For the rest of their days they would carry a deep sorrow within their hearts.

VIATOR   NIA   INVIA PROCVA

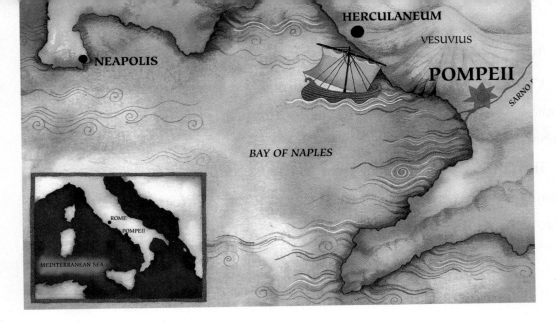

The Story of Pompeii

Before the eruption of Mount Vesuvius, Pompeii was a busy, beautiful Roman city where about 15,000 people lived. In those days, during the ancient Roman Empire, Vesuvius appeared green and peaceful, but on August 24 in A.D. 79, a great mushroom-shaped cloud rose from its top and, to everyone's surprise, the volcano began to erupt. In nearby Pompeii, day became as dark as night. Showers of ash and stone fell, covering streets and houses. Within a few hours rooftops started to collapse, and many people fled. The next morning, clouds of poisonous gases and ash poured down from the volcano, suffocating those who had stayed behind.

When the dust had settled, Pompeii and its lovely surroundings, including the neighboring city of Herculaneum, had disappeared beneath a blanket of ash, pumice, and lava. The city had become like Sleeping Beauty's castle. Trees and plants grew over it. As time passed, people remembered the city of Pompeii, but they forgot exactly where it had been. Pompeii slept for nearly 1,700 years, until, in 1748, excavators began to find its remains. Temples, theaters, baths, shops, and beautifully painted houses were uncovered, along with skeletons of the victims, sometimes in family groups. Soon Pompeii became famous, and people came from far and wide to see it. They were amazed at what they saw.

In 1863 the archaeologist Giuseppe Fiorelli decided to try an experiment. He noticed that where a body had lain in the ash, it had left hollows in the shape of the body that had once been there. He poured plaster into one body space and waited for it to set. When the ashes around it were removed, he found that he was left with a plaster cast in the exact shape of the victim's body. Since then, many casts have been made and can be seen in Pompeii—sad reminders of the city's fate.

Vesuvius has not erupted since March 1944, but the volcano is not dead—only sleeping. Like all volcanoes, it has given the land around it rich soil that is easy to farm. As in Roman times, the people of modern-day Italy have built their homes there, and towns and villages crowd the shores of the Bay of Naples. One day Vesuvius will erupt again, but now, with modern scientific instruments checking the volcano each day, it is hoped that no more lives will be lost.

Pompeii is not yet fully excavated, but its uncovered remains help us see what a Roman city really looked like and how the Romans lived, worked, and played.

ISLANDS

by Marilyn Singer

Dad likes to talk
            about islands—
how they sink
how they rise
How some are bred
            by volcanoes
and others built from coral bones
How some are crowned by castles
and some stripped clean
            even of trees
It's the earth playing peek-a-boo
            with the sea, he says
But to me it sounds
            a more dangerous game
And I think once in a while the sea
            just finds it amusing
                  to let the earth
                        win

Instructions for the Earth's Dishwasher

by Lisa Westberg Peters

Please set the
continental plates
gently on the
continental shelves.
No jostling or scraping.

Please stack the
basins right side up.
No tilting or turning
upside-down.

Please scrape the mud
out of the mud pots.
But watch out!
They're still hot.

As for the forks
in the river,
just let them soak.

Remember,
if anything breaks,
it's your fault.

NATURAL DISASTERS

by Marilyn Singer

We were talking disasters
    scaring ourselves
        with what on earth would scare us:
Volcanoes venting red-hot rivers
        spumes of ash
    like barbecues gone crazy
Earthquakes that crack the world
    like a walnut
Sandstorms that suffocate
Tidal waves that drown
    Hurricanes, tornadoes
    avalanches, floods
And blizzards
    simple blizzards—
those frightened me the most
    trapping me right there in my house
        with nothing to eat
    but my shoes
We were talking disasters
    feeling the earth go wobbly
    leaving ourselves
        with no place to hide
Until right outside my window
    a robin chirruped loudly
        in the hickory tree
like nothing on earth mattered
    but its song
And suddenly the room righted itself
    the floor held steady
and we knew that we were safe
        for at least another day

LIVING WITH LAVA

by Lisa Westberg Peters

Lava.
It squeezes out of a volcano
like fiery black toothpaste.
It buries a road,
a parking lot,
and a wall.

Lava.
It steams
in the tropical rain.
It hardens
in the Hawaiian heat.

Lava.
Machines with grinding wheels
crush it,
and bulldozers with wide blades
push it.

Lava.
Men and women
in work boots and hard hats
mix it with tar.
They build a road,
a parking lot,
and a wall.

Lava.
It squeezes out of a volcano.

CENTER OF THE EARTH

by Marilyn Singer

No matter how snowy the Wyoming plains
　　how icy the Iceland hills
　　how chilly the Atlantic waters
No matter how frigid the spot,
　　it sits atop a bubbling cauldron of molten rock
　　that finds a way to shoot up
　　　　streams of glowing lava, jets of steamy water,
　　　　　　fountains of sky-high fire, bursts of boiling mud,
reminding us that the earth's deep pot
　　is always cooking
　　always hot.

MOUNT SAINT HELENS WASHINGTON

by Diane Siebert

Gone the fire, gone the roar;
Mount Saint Helens sleeps once more.
Silent, steamless, still for now,
But someday—
　　rumble . . .
　　　　belch . . .
　　　　　　KER-PLOW!!!

But wait! The sleeping lady stirs!
That sudden, steaming sigh is hers;
She wakes and quakes, her ashy plume
Foreshadowing the big
　　　　KA-BOOM!!!

MOUNT ST. HELENS On May 18, 1980, the 9,677-foot-tall peak in the Cascade Range erupted after being dormant since 1857. The entire north face of the mountain was blown away. The blast moved at 300 miles per hour with temperatures of more than 600 degrees Fahrenheit. More than 100 square miles of forest were obliterated by landslides, and entire towns, rivers, and lakes were covered with a blanket of ash, rock, and mud. Volcanic ash spewed 15 miles into the atmosphere and spread for hundreds of miles, blotting out the sun. When it was over, the top 1,300 feet of the mountain lay scattered on the valley floor and 57 people along with countless animals had been killed. Then in September 2004, after years of dozing, St. Helens awoke again with thousands of small earthquakes, plumes of steam and ash, and a flow of molten rock that reached the surface and began to form a new dome inside the crater.

COYOTE SCHOOL NEWS

JOAN SANDIN

Rancho San Isidro

My name is Ramón Ernesto Ramírez, but everybody calls me Monchi. I live on a ranch that my great-grandfather built a long time ago when this land was part of Mexico. That was before the United States bought it and moved the line in 1854. My father has a joke about that. He says my great-grandfather was an *americano*, not because he crossed the line, but because the line crossed him.

In my family we are six kids: me, my big brother Junior, my big sister Natalia, my little tattletale brother Victor, my little sister Loli, and the baby Pili. My *tío* Chaco lives with us too. He is the youngest brother of my father.

The real name of our ranch is Rancho San Isidro, after the patron saint of my great-grandfather, but most of the time everybody calls it the Ramírez Ranch.

On our ranch we have chickens and pigs and cattle and horses. The boys in the Ramírez family know how to ride and rope. We are a family of *vaqueros*. In the fall and spring we have roundup on our ranch. Many people come to help with the cattle and the horses. Those are the most exciting days of the year, even more exciting than Christmas.

The things I don't like about our ranch are always having to get the wood for the fire, and the long and bumpy ride to school.

My tío Chaco drives the school bus.

"It's not fair," I tell him. "We have to get up earlier than all the other kids at Coyote School and we get home the latest too."

"Don't forget," says my tío, "you get first choice of seats."

Ha, ha. By the time the last kid gets in, we are all squeezed together like sardines in a can. And the bus is shaking and bumping like it has a flat tire.

"I wish President Roosevelt would do something about these roads," I tell my tío.

"Hey, you know how to write English," he says. "Write him a letter."

"Maybe I will," I say.

---

americano (AH-mair-ee-CAHN-oh)—American
tío (TEE-oh)—uncle
rancho (RAHN-choe)—ranch
san (sahn)—saint
vaqueros (bah-CARE-rose)—cowboys

Coyote School

"*Mira, mira,* Monchi," Natalia says, pinching my cheek. "There's your little *novia.*"

She means Rosie. I like Rosie, but I hate it when Natalia teases me. Rosie lives at Coyote Ranch, close enough to school that she can walk. Always she waits by the road so she can race the bus.

"*¡Ándale! ¡Ándale!* Hurry up!" we yell at my tío Chaco, but every time he lets her win.

Rosie wasn't first today anyway. Lalo and Frankie were. Their horses are standing in the shade of the big mesquite tree.

Yap! Yap! Yap! Always Chipito barks when he sees us, and Miss Byers says, "Hush, Chipito!" Then she smiles and waves at us.

Miss Byers is new this year. Her ranch is a hundred miles from here, in Rattlesnake Canyon, so five days of the week she and Chipito live in the little room behind the school. All of us like Miss Byers, even the big kids, because she is young and nice and fair. We like that she lives on a ranch, and we like her swell ideas:

1. Baseball at recess,
2. The Perfect Attendance Award,
3. *Coyote News.*

mira (MEER-ah)—look
novia (NOVE-ee-ah)—girlfriend
ándale (AHN-dah-lay)—come on; hurry up

Coyote News

All week we have been working on our first *Coyote News*. Natalia made up the name, and Joey drew the coyote. First we looked at some other newspapers: the *Arizona Daily Star*, *Western Livestock Journal*, and *Little Cowpuncher*. That one we liked best because all the stories and pictures were done by kids.

"Monchi," said Loli, "put me cute."

"What?" I said. Sometimes it's not easy to understand my little sister's English.

"Miss Byers says you have to help me put words to my story," she said.

"Okay," I told her. "But I have my own story to do, so hurry up and learn to write."

Loli's story was *muy tonta*, but one thing was good. She remembered how to write all the words I spelled for her.

Even if Victor is my brother, I have to say he is a big tattletale—*chismoso*. When Gilbert was writing his story for *Coyote News*, Victor told on him for writing in Spanish.

But Miss Byers did not get mad at Gilbert. She smiled at him! And then she said Spanish is a beautiful language that people around here have been speaking for hundreds of years, and that we should be proud we can speak it too!

Ha ha, Victor, you big chismoso!

When we finished our stories and pictures, Miss Byers cut a stencil for the mimeograph. Then she printed copies of *Coyote News* for us to take home, and we hung them up on the ceiling to dry the ink. My tío Chaco said it looked like laundry day at Coyote School.

muy (MOO-ee)—very
tonta (TONE-tah)—silly
chismoso (cheese-MOE-soe)—tattletale
señor (sin-YORE)—Mr.
grandote (grahn-DOE-tay)—great, big, huge

Issue Number One   September 15, 1938

COYOTE NEWS

Stories and Pictures by the Students of Coyote School, Pima County, Arizona

Something New at Coyote School

Coyote News was the idea of our teacher, but we write the stories and draw the pictures. The big kids help the little kids...Rosie Garcia, Grade 3

About Coyote School

This year we have 12 kids and all the grades except Grade 5...Billy Mills, Grade 3

We Ride Our Horses to School

The road to Rancho del Cerro is a very big problem for the bus of Mr. Ramirez. For that reason Lalo and I ride our horses to school--16 miles all the days. The year past it was 2,352 miles. We had to put new shoes on the horses 5 times...Frankie Lopez, Grade 6

Ándale Ándale We want to go home

by Lalo Lopez

The Perfect Attendance

Miss Byers will give a prize to anybody who comes to school all the days, no matter what. The prize is called The Perfect Attendance Award and it is a silver dollar! For me perfect attendance is not easy, but oh boy, I would like to win that silver dollar............Monchi Ramirez, Grade 4

Yap! Yap!

by Cynthia

Chipito

The dog of the teacher is called Chipito. He is very cute. He likes Loli best.....story by Loli Ramirez, Grade 1 with help by Monchi Ramirez, Grade 4

Señor Grandote

Our bus driver ran over a big rattlesnake. We took the skin and gave it to our teacher. She measured him with the yardstick. He was 5 feet and 7 inches! She hung him on the wall next to President Roosevelt. We kids call him Señor Grandote because in Spanish it means Mr. Huge................Gilbert Perez, Grade 6

Señor Grandote

by Joey Brown

Chiles

Every day I am asking my father when we will have roundup. He says I am making him *loco* with my nagging and that first we have to pick *todos los chiles*.

All of us kids are tired of picking the chiles. It doesn't matter that we get home late from school, we still have to do it. And then, before the chiles dry out, we have to string them to make the *sartas*.

Last night we were taking about 600 pounds of the chiles to my tío Enrique's ranch. I was in the back of the truck when it hit a big rock.

All the heavy sacks fell on me. Oh boy, it hurt so much!

But I did not tell my father. He had told me not to ride in the back of the truck, and I was afraid he would be mad.

My hand was still hurting this morning when Miss Byers did Fingernail Inspection.

"Monchi," she said, "what happened to your wrist? It's all black-and-blue and swollen."

"The chiles fell on him," Victor told her. "My father told him not to ride in the back."

"¡Chismoso!" I hissed at him.

Miss Byers called my tío Chaco over, and they had a long talk.

"Back in the bus, *mi'jo*," my tío said. "I have to take you to Tucson."

"Tucson!" I said. "Why?"

"You got to see the doctor," he said. So we drove all the way to Tucson to my *tía* Lena's house. At first my aunt was surprised and happy to see us, but then my *tío* told her why we were there.

"Monchi!" my *tía* said. "*¡Pobrecito!*" Then she told my *tío* Chaco to go back with the bus and she would take care of me.

My *tía* took me to a doctor. He moved my hand around. It hurt when he did that.

"I'm afraid the wrist is broken," he told my *tía*. "I need to set it and put it in a cast."

So I got a cast of plaster on my arm, and I had to stay in Tucson. But for me that was no problem! My *tía* felt very sorry for me. She cooked my favorite foods, and I got to pick the stations on her radio. That night Miss Byers called on the telephone to ask about me. She said she would come early Monday morning to drive me to school.

On Sunday my *tía* took me to the Tarzan picture show at the Fox Theater. It was swell! After the show we got ice cream and walked around downtown to look in the windows of the stores. I saw many things I liked. The best was a silver buckle with a hole to put a silver dollar. *¡Ay caramba!* I wish I had a buckle like that.

loco (LOW-coe)—crazy

todos (TOE-dose)—all

los (lohs)—the

chiles (CHEE-less)—chile peppers

sartas (SAR-tahs)—strings of chile peppers

mi'jo (MEE-hoe)—my son, sonny

tía (TEE-ah)—aunt

pobrecito (pobe-ray-SEE-toe)—poor little thing

¡ay caramba! (EYE car-RAHM-bah)—oh boy!

Nochebuena

For *Nochebuena* we are many people. Some are family I see only at Christmas and roundup and weddings and funerals. The day before Nochebuena my cousins from Sonora arrived. Now we could make the *piñata*!

First we cut the strips of red, white, and green paper. Then we paste them on a big *olla*. When the piñata is ready, we give it to my mother to fill with the *dulces* she hides in her secret places.

On Nochebuena, Junior and my tío Chaco hung the piñata between two big mesquite trees and we kids lined up to hit it, the littlest ones first. My mother tied a *mascada* over my little brother Pili's eyes and my tía Lena turned him around and around. She gave him the stick and pointed him toward the piñata. My tío Chaco and Junior made it easy for him. They did not jerk on the rope when he swung.

"¡Dale! ¡Dale!" we were yelling, but Pili never came close. None of the little kids could hit it. Then it was Loli's turn.

BAM.

Some peanuts fell out. Gilbert and I dived to get them. One by one, the other kids tried and missed. Then it was Natalia's turn. She took a good swing and—*BAM.*

The piñata broke open, and all the kids were in the dirt, screaming and laughing and picking up gum and nuts and oranges and candies.

Just before midnight we got into my tío Chaco's bus and my father's pickup to go to the Mass at Amado. When we got home my mother and my tías put out *tamales* and *menudo* and *tortillas* and cakes and coffee and other drinks. We had music and dancing. Nobody told us we had to go to bed.

Sometime in the night Santa Claus came and gave us our presents. Junior got a pair of spurs, Victor got a big red top, and Loli got a little toy dog that looks like Chipito. But I got the best present. It was a silver-dollar buckle, the one I had seen with my tía Lena in Tucson. It doesn't have a dollar yet, only a hole, but when I win the Perfect Attendance I will put my silver dollar in that hole.

Nochebuena (No-chay-BUAY-nah)—Christmas Eve

piñata (peen-YAH-tah)—clay pot (olla) filled with treats

olla (OY-yah)—clay pot

dulces (DOOL-sehss)—sweets, candy

mascada (mas-KAH-dah)—scarf

¡dale! (DAH-lay)—hit it!

tamales (tah-MAH-less)—steamed, filled dough

menudo (men-OO-doe)—tripe soup

tortillas (tor-TEE-yahs)—flat Mexican bread

Issue Number Five   January 12, 1939

COYOTE NEWS

Happy New Year!

Stories and Pictures by the Students of Coyote School, Pima County, Arizona

Miss Byers' Radio

Miss Byers brought her new radio to school. It has a big battery, so it doesn't matter that Coyote School has no electricity. We got to hear President Roosevelt's speech to the Congress. He told them to be prepared for war. Then he said, "Happy New Year."........Monchi Ramirez, Grade 4

Our President

waw

by Joey Brown

Our President's Voice

None of us kids had heard the President's voice before. When he said "war" it sounded like "waw." We were all laughing because we never heard anybody who talked like that, but Billy said some of the dudes do.............Rosie Garcia, Grade 3

Some Noisy Children

When the President was talking, Loli was noisy. Miss Byers gave her peanuts to make her quiet. I was quiet without the peanuts...Victor, Grade 2

Yap!

By Frankie Lopez

Music on the Radio

We got to listen to the music on Miss Byers' radio. She has many stations, but I liked best to hear the one with the rancheras..........Gilbert Perez, Grade 6

No Earrings for Christmas

Santa Claus didn't bring me any earrings. Loli says it's because he knows that I don't have any holes in my ears like she does......Cynthia Brown, Grade 2

The Perfect Attendance Report

Miss Byers says Santa Claus must have given some of our kids the flu and chicken pox for Christmas. The only kids who still have perfect attendance are Natalia, Monchi, Victor, and me..........Billy Mills, Grade 3

La Fiesta de los Vaqueros Rodeo Parade

We are so excited because Miss Byers just told us something wonderful. Our school gets to be in the Tucson Rodeo Parade!...Natalia Ramirez, Grade 8

Roundup!

The vaqueros were hollering, "¡Ándale! ¡Ándale!" They were cutting through the cattle on their horses, swinging their lassoes in the air to rope out the steers. My tío Chaco threw his saddle up on his horse, Canelo, and joined them. We kids clapped and whistled. Sometimes we helped my father or my tíos. We brought them rope or a fresh horse or something to drink.

That night we boys got to eat with the vaqueros and sit by the fire and listen to them play their guitars and sing their *rancheras*. We got to hear their exciting stories and their bragging and their bad words. When my father came over to Junior and me, I thought he was going to tell us to go in to bed, but instead he said, "Tomorrow I want you boys to help with the branding." Junior had helped since he was eleven, but it was the first time my father had ever asked me.

"Tomorrow I have school," I said.

"School!" said Junior. "Monchi, don't you understand? You get to help with the branding!"

"He doesn't want to lose the Perfect Attendance," said Victor.

"The Perfect Attendance!" said Junior. "Monchi, you are crazier than a goat. You are a Ramírez. We are a family of vaqueros. Roundup is more important than the Perfect Attendance."

I knew Junior was right, but I touched the empty hole of my silver-dollar buckle and I sighed. Adiós, Perfect Attendance.

For two exciting days Junior and I helped with the roundup. First the vaqueros lassoed the calves and wrestled them down to the ground. Then Junior and I held them while my father and my tío Enrique branded them and cut the ears and gave them the shot.

¡Qué barullo! The red-hot irons were smoking, and the burned hair was stinking. The calves were fighting and bawling like giant babies. They were much heavier than Junior and me. It was hard work and dangerous to hold them down. I got dust in my eyes and in my nose, but I didn't care.

After the work of the roundup was over, we made the fiesta! First was a race for the kids. We had to ride as fast as we could to the chuck wagon, take an orange, and ride back again. Junior won on Pinto. He got a big jar of candies and gave some to all of us. Last came Victor and his little *burro.* All that day we had races and roping contests.

That night we had a big *barbacoa.* The kids got cold soda pops. When the music started, all the vaqueros wanted to dance with Natalia. The one they call Chapo asked her to be his novia, but Natalia told him she doesn't want to get married. She wants to go to high school.

Monday morning when we left for school, the vaqueros were packing their bedrolls. We waved and hollered from our bus, *"¡Adiós! ¡Adios! ¡Hasta la vista!"*

———————— ————————

rancheras (rahn-CHAIR-ahs)—Mexican folk songs
fiesta (fee-ESS-tah)—party, celebration
de (day)—of
adios (ah-DYOHSS)—good-bye
qué (kaye)—what, how
barullo (bah-ROO-yoe)—noise, racket
burro (BOOR-row)—donkey
barbacoa (bar-bah-KOH-ah)—barbecue
hasta la vista (AH-stah lah VEE-stah)—see you

71

COYOTE NEWS

¡Hasta la vista!

Stories and Pictures by the Students of Coyote School, Pima County, Arizona

Adios Coyote School!

Lalo   Natalia

Good-bye, everybody! Thank you, Miss Byers!

by Lalo Lopez

Eduardo (Lalo) and Natalia Graduate!

Lalo and I have passed the Eighth Grade Standard Achievement Test! I am happy to graduate and I am excited about high school, but I will miss my teacher and all the kids at my dear Coyote School...Natalia Ramirez, Grade 8

I Lose the Perfect Attendance

I was absent from school to help with the roundup. It was very exciting, but now it is over and I am feeling sad. The vaqueros are gone and I will not get a silver dollar for my buckle....Monchi Ramirez, Grade 4

The Perfect Attendance Report

The only one who still has perfect attendance is Victor. Even Miss Byers has been absent, because when it was roundup on her ranch a big calf stepped on her foot. We had Miss Elias for 3 days. Miss Byers had to pay her 5 dollars a day to take her place.....Gilbert Perez, Grade 6

Please forgive me, Miss Byers

300 pounds

BY Rosie Garcia

A Visit to the Boston Beans

Mr. and Mrs. Bean invited my family to visit them this summer in Boston. Boston is Back East. It is even bigger than Tucson. No other kid at Coyote School has ever gone that far away!.............Billy Mills, Grade 3

Earrings

My daddy is getting married. Joey and I will get a new mother and 4 new brothers. Laura is nice and she can cook, but the best part is she has pierced ears and now I will get to have them too!....Cynthia Brown, Grade 2

Last Issue for the School Year

This is the last issue before the summer vacation. I am saving all my Coyote News newspapers so that someday I can show my children all the swell and exciting things we did at Coyote School..........Rosie Garcia, Grade 3

The Last Day of School

On the last day of school Miss Byers gave us a fiesta with cupcakes and candies and Cracker Jacks and soda pops. We got to listen to Mexican music on her radio. I didn't have to dance with Natalia. I got to dance with Rosie.

Then Miss Byers turned off the radio and stood in the front of the room between President Roosevelt and Señor Grandote. She called Natalia and Lalo up to the front and told them how proud we were that they were graduates of Coyote School, and how much we would miss them. We all clapped and whistled.

Next, Miss Byers gave Edelia a paper and said, "Please read what it says, Edelia."

Edelia read: "Edelia Ortiz has been promoted to Grade Two." Miss Byers had to help her to read "promoted," but we all clapped and cheered anyway. Edelia looked very happy and proud.

Then Miss Byers asked Victor to come to the front of the room, and I knew what that meant. I didn't want to listen when she said how good it was that he had not missed a day of school, and I didn't want to look when she gave him the silver dollar. I knew I should be happy that Victor won the Perfect Attendance, but I was not.

"And now, boys and girls," Miss Byers said, "it's time for the next award."

"What next award?" we asked.

"The *Coyote News* Writing Award for the student who has contributed most to *Coyote News* by writing his own stories and by helping others write theirs. The winner of the *Coyote News* Writing Award is Ramón Ernesto Ramírez."

"Me?" I said.

All the kids were clapping and whistling. I just sat there.

"Go up to the front," Natalia said and gave me a push.

Miss Byers smiled and shook my hand. "Congratulations, Monchi," she said, and then she gave me the award.

¡Ay caramba! The Coyote News Writing Award was a shiny silver dollar!

"Oh thank you, Miss Byers!" I said. "*¡Gracias!*" I was so surprised and happy. I pushed the silver dollar into the round hole on my buckle. It fit perfectly!

"*¡Muy hermosa!*" Miss Byers said.

She was right. It was very beautiful.

gracias (GRAHS-see-ahs)—thank you
hermosa (air-MOE-sah)—beautiful

73

CHARLOTTE HERMAN

MAX MALONE
Makes a Million

Illustrated by Cat Bowman Smith

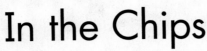

In the Chips

Max Malone was lying on the living-room floor. He was reading the Sunday comics and laughing at the latest adventures of Garfield.

His sister Rosalie was working on a crossword puzzle at the dining-room table. "Does anyone know a five-letter word that ends in *t* and means 'silent'?"

"Quiet!" Max ordered. "I'm trying to read."

"'Quiet'! That's it! Thanks, Max."

Mrs. Malone was on the couch, reading the other parts of the paper. She especially liked the human-interest stories. Those were the stories about dogs who saved entire families from burning buildings. Or firemen who rescued cats from trees.

"Now, this is interesting," said Mrs. Malone. "A ten-year-old boy made a fortune selling chocolate-chip cookies."

Max looked up from the comics and listened as his mother read:

TEN-YEAR-OLD IN THE CHIPS

"Ten-year-old Anthony Baker of Portland, Oregon, doesn't have to steal cookies from the cookie jar. He puts them there. And judging by the number of cookies he's baked using his own original recipe, he's been filling lots of cookie jars.

"Anthony doesn't know exactly how many cookies he's baked so far. He's not counting. He's too busy counting the money he's making."

"Let me see that," said Max, jumping to his feet. He hurried over to the couch and sat down next to his mother. She handed him the paper, and he began reading silently. He interrupted himself with lots of "Wow"s and "Oh, boy"s.

"Wow! All he did was buy an old stove. And he rented an old shack in his neighborhood, where he baked and sold the cookies." Max continued to read to himself, until he came to the last line. "Oh, boy, listen to what it says here: 'This young man may well be on his way to becoming a millionaire.' "

Max tossed the newspaper onto the couch. "Wow! A millionaire, just by baking and selling chocolate-chip cookies. I could do that." He had watched his mother bake cookies lots of times. There was nothing to it. "I could get an old stove and rent a shack somewhere."

"There aren't any shacks around here," Rosalie informed him.

Max thought this over. Rosalie was right. He couldn't remember seeing any shacks in his neighborhood.

"Then I'll just use our kitchen. We've got an old stove." He ran into the kitchen to check out the stove. Rosalie followed him. Max opened and closed the oven door and worked the control knob a couple of times.

"This stove should work out even better. I already know how to use it. All I have to do is get Gordy to help me."

"I'll help you too," said Rosalie. "You'll need all the help you can get."

That's just what Max didn't need. Rosalie's help. She loved to eat anything that was sweet. She could eat tons of sugared cereal and never get tired of it. He could just imagine what she'd do with his cookies.

"No thanks," said Max. "You'd eat them faster than we could bake them."

"I'm not sure about this cookie business of yours," said Mrs. Malone, coming into the kitchen to pour herself a cup of coffee. "I don't like the idea of your fooling around with the stove. And the mess…"

"Come on, Mom. What if Anthony Baker's mother told him not to fool around with the stove and worried about making a mess? He never would've made his fortune."

Mrs. Malone leaned against the counter, took a sip of coffee, and sighed deeply. "Oh, well. I guess I ought to let you give it a try. Twenty years from now I don't want you to come to me and tell me that I kept you from becoming a millionaire. Just be careful."

With an air of victory, Max raised his arms and shook his fists, the way he had seen athletes in the Olympics do. "All riiiight! Just you wait and see, Mom. We'll make so much money, you won't have to sell any more memo pads." Mrs. Malone sold personalized memo pads through the mail.

"I'd better go call Gordy," said Max, running to the phone.

Max punched in Gordy's number and waited for someone to answer. He hoped it wouldn't be Gordy's mother or father. He hated talking to parents on the phone and having to be polite.

Luckily it was Gordy who finally answered, and Max didn't waste any time on small talk. He got straight to the point.

"Gordy, get over here right away. You, pal, are about to make your fortune!"

Quality Ingredients

"**E**ggs," Gordy called out.

"Check," answered Max.

"Flour."

"Check."

"Sugar."

"Check."

Gordy continued to read off the list of ingredients on the back of the package of chocolate chips, while Max checked to see what was in stock in his kitchen.

"Baking soda," Gordy read on.

"No baking soda," said Max. "But we've got baking powder."

"Good enough," said Gordy. "Okay, that's everything on the list. We're all set." Gordy was just as excited as Max was about making a million dollars, and was anxious to start their business. He had wasted no time in getting over to Max's house.

"Then let's do it," said Max as he preheated the oven to 375°, the way his mother always did when she baked cookies.

"Hey, wait a minute," interrupted Rosalie, who had been standing by watching and hoping to be asked for help. "You can't use that recipe. What's the point? Anyone can bake those cookies. You need an original recipe. Like Anthony Baker had."

Max tucked his chin in the space between his thumb and index finger and did some heavy thinking.

"Rosalie is right," he said finally. "We've got to change the recipe by adding some other ingredients too."

"May I make a suggestion?" asked Mrs. Malone, who had gotten off the phone just in time to hear that last remark. "First bake the cookies using the recipe on the back of the package. Then once you get it perfect, you can vary it here and there and do a little experimenting."

"That'll take too much time," said Max. "We want to get started on the baking right away." He took out two bowls, measuring cups and spoons, and his mother's electric hand mixer.

While Gordy began combining the flour, baking powder, and salt in one bowl, Max measured the white and brown sugars, butter, and vanilla into the other.

"Oops!" said Gordy. "I seem to have lost some flour."

Max looked up from his bowl to see Gordy enveloped in a cloud of all-purpose flour. He also noticed that there was more flour on the counter and on the floor than there was in the bowl.

"That's okay," said Max. "Just add some more."

"I don't know how much I spilled."

"Guess," said Max. "What's the difference? It's an original recipe anyway."

"I think I'd better leave," said Mrs. Malone, touching her hand to her forehead and hurrying out of the kitchen.

"What now?" asked Gordy.

"It's time to add our original ingredients," said Max. He opened up the refrigerator and discovered a jar of honey. He held it up for Gordy to see. "Like honey, for instance."

"Honey is good," said Gordy. "It's a quality ingredient. My father says we should use only quality ingredients in our cookies. People appreciate quality in a product and won't settle for less."

"Yogurt is quality," came a voice that could no longer keep quiet. From where she was sitting, on a stool in a corner of the kitchen, Rosalie began to throw out suggestions. "Cinnamon is quality. So are nutmeg, and cloves, and ginger."

"I was getting to that," said Max.

"And add more brown sugar. It'll give the cookies a rich, golden appearance."

Max added cinnamon, nutmeg, cloves, ginger, and an extra cup of brown sugar. "I think that's enough original ingredients." He picked up the mixer, positioned the beaters in the bowl and pushed the switch to low.

"Hey," Max called above the noise of the mixer. "There's something wrong here. It's not beating right."

"You forgot the eggs," Rosalie shouted to him.

"Oh, right." Max turned off the mixer and added two eggs according to the recipe, and one more because of all the extra ingredients. He started up the mixer again on high.

All the quality ingredients shot up in the air and splattered all over the counter and all over Max. He set the speed to medium and tried again. Everything blended together smoothly. He gradually added Gordy's flour mixture.

"This is easy enough," said Max as he and Gordy dropped spoonfuls of the mixture onto two ungreased cookie sheets. They placed the cookies in the oven and peered through the window of the oven door to watch them bake. Rosalie licked the batter from the bowl.

"Oops," said Gordy. "I think there is something seriously wrong with these chocolate-chip cookies."

"What?" asked Max.

"We forgot the chocolate chips."

Max slapped his forehead. "I can't believe it. We forgot the most important ingredient."

"Oh, well," said Gordy. "This will be our practice batch."

Rosalie pushed Max and Gordy aside so she could look through the window. "I think you'll need lots of practice. The cookies aren't rising. They're flat. Like pancakes."

"Two very large pancakes," said Max, as he watched the batter run together.

When the cookie-pancakes began turning brown around the edges, Max took the cookie sheets out of the oven. "We'd better try again. Only this time we'll double the recipe. And we'll use the recipe on the back of the package. We've wasted too much time already."

While Rosalie was nibbling on the practice cookies, Max and Gordy combined all the ingredients in two larger bowls. This time they remembered to add the chocolate chips.

They took out extra baking pans from the cabinet and dropped spoonfuls of batter onto them. "These should work," said Max, placing the pans in the oven. "Now let's figure out how much to sell them for." He took a pencil from the drawer, and a pad of paper that said *From the desk of MAX MALONE*. Then he and Gordy sat down at the kitchen table.

"All right," said Max, as he doodled on the pad. "How should we sell them? By the cookie or by the pound?"

"The shop in the mall sells them by the pound," Rosalie offered. "Mmm. Semi-sweet chocolate chips with macadamia nuts. I can taste them now."

"I like the white chocolate with macadamia nuts," said Gordy.

"Come on, you guys," said Max. "You're wasting time."

The doorbell rang. It was Austin Healy, from across the street. He was just six years old, and didn't even care that his father had named him after a car.

"Something smells good in here," said Austin, sniffing the air.

"It's our cookies," said Max. "We're going into the cookie business. We're going to make a million."

"Can I go into business with you?" Austin asked. "I'd like to make a million too."

"You're too young," said Max. "This is a real business. We're not just playing. Maybe when you're older."

"Are you going into the pancake business too?" Austin asked, glancing at Rosalie, who was eating the cookie-pancakes.

"Oh, that," said Max. "That was just our practice batch."

"I think you've got two practice batches," said Rosalie. "Your cookies are burning."

Max and Gordy made a dash for the oven. "Oh, no!" said Max as he began taking out the pans. "They're ruined."

Instead of being golden brown, the cookies were a very dark brown with black around the edges.

"I guess you'll have to try again," said Austin.

"We've already tried twice," said Gordy. "I don't think I can handle a third time."

"We're all out of ingredients anyway," said Max. He slumped into his chair. He wondered if Anthony Baker had had all this trouble.

"I think," said Austin as he helped himself to a piece of Rosalie's cookie-pancakes, "I think you should go into another business. Do something you know how to do." He helped himself to a second piece and walked out the door.

Big Business

"What do we know how to do?" Gordy asked Max.

"Nothing," Max answered.

They were resting on Max's front steps after cleaning up Mrs. Malone's kitchen. Max was trying to figure out where he had gone wrong, and where Anthony Baker had gone right. Maybe Anthony had an older stove. Or a better recipe.

"We'd better think of something fast," said Gordy. "Vacation is over in two weeks."

Max sighed deeply. Then he shut his eyes and tried to think of something he knew how to do. Something he knew about. He knew about garage sales. One of his favorite things to do was to buy lots of great junk at Mrs. Filbert's garage sales. Mrs. Filbert was Max's neighbor. Max and Gordy could have a garage sale. The problem was, Max didn't have a garage. Neither did Gordy.

The door swung open and out came Mrs. Malone with two glasses of lemonade. "Here, boys. I think you can use this."

"Hey, thanks," said Max and Gordy, taking the glasses from her. They gulped down their drinks.

"Boy, this lemonade hits the spot," said Gordy.

"Lemonade!" shouted Max, jumping to his feet. "That's it. We'll make our millions in lemonade."

"Are you kidding? We tried to sell the stuff lots of times. Rosalie drank most of it. She charged it and never paid us back. We didn't make a single penny."

"We weren't running a real business before," said Max. "We were just fooling around. Besides, do you have any better ideas?"

"No," answered Gordy.

"Then we'll sell lemonade," said Max. "It's easy to make. And it's cheap." He could just picture it. First they would sell lemonade from a stand. And when they became real successful, they would go on to big business. They could sell frozen lemonade in a supermarket. Or fresh, in cartons.

The next day Max and Gordy set up their lemonade stand in the park. Max had a pitcher filled with lemonade made from fresh lemons. He had added sugar little by little, until he got it to taste just right. He topped it all off with ice cubes. Gordy brought a small folding table, two chairs, and paper cups. They hung a sign from the table. It read:

LEMONADE
25 cents

"Business should be real good," said Max. "It's going to be a hot day."

They sat down at the table. They tried to look very businesslike while they waited for their first customer.

Soon their first customer was walking toward them. It was Rosalie.

"I'd like to try some of your lemonade," she said.

"That will be twenty-five cents," said Max.

"Charge it," said Rosalie.

"Cash only," said Max.

Rosalie hesitated for a moment. Then she dug into her pocket and came up with a quarter. She plunked it down on the table. Max and Gordy exchanged smiles. They were proud of how businesslike they were acting. Max poured some lemonade into a cup and watched her drink it.

"Just as I thought," she said. "It isn't sweet enough." She turned to leave. "Maybe I'll bring you some more sugar later."

What Max and Gordy needed were more customers. At this rate, Max's mother would be selling memo pads forever. "The park is so empty today," said Max.

"Probably because of the heat," said Gordy.

"I sure am thirsty," said Max.

"Me too," said Gordy.

"I've been thinking," said Max. "Maybe we should taste the lemonade again. To see if Rosalie is right about the sugar."

"Good idea," said Gordy. "We don't want to sell sour lemonade."

Each poured himself a cup and drank it down in one gulp.

"It's sweet enough for me," said Max.

"Plenty sweet," said Gordy. "Let's try a little more. Just to be sure."

After the second cup, they waited for more customers. The sun was beating down on them. The ice cubes were beginning to melt. They poured themselves some more lemonade.

"It's only right that we taste it again," said Max. "To see if melted ice cubes affect the flavor."

They drank the lemonade and decided that it was still sweet enough. Then they waited some more.

Finally three small boys followed by their mother ran into the park.

"At last," said Max.

"This is it," said Gordy.

"Hey, lemonade!" the oldest boy shouted.

"Yay, lemonade!" shouted the younger ones. And all three ran toward Max and Gordy.

"An easy seventy-five cents," said Max.

"Maybe even a dollar," said Gordy when he saw the mother coming after her sons.

"We want lemonade," the boys told their mother.

"Not now," she said.

"But we're thirsty."

"We don't know what's in it," she whispered as she led them away.

Max and Gordy were angry. And insulted.

"What does she think is in here, anyway?" asked Max.

"Yeah," said Gordy. "Poison?"

They poured themselves some more lemonade and drank it. They wanted the mother to see them drinking it. She would see that it wasn't poisoned. Besides, they were thirsty. And hot. The ice cubes had melted completely.

"This tastes like sour water," said Max.

"Yeah," said Gordy. "Warm sour water. It's definitely not quality."

"It needs more sugar," said Max.

By the time Rosalie came back with some sugar, Max and Gordy were ready to leave.

"How was business?" asked Rosalie.

"Slow," said Max.

"Too bad," said Rosalie. "Austin is making a fortune."

"Austin is selling lemonade?" asked Max.

"Yes. Two kinds. One made with sugar, and one with Sweet 'n Low. Remember when we saw those men chopping up that sidewalk on Friday?" She began adding sugar to the lemonade.

"Yeah," said Max. "In front of the post office."

"Well, today they're pouring cement for the new sidewalk. And that's where Austin is." She sat down at the table and little by little drank up the rest of the lemonade.

They took apart the stand and dropped everything off at Max's house. Then they hurried over to the post office.

Sure enough, there was Austin selling lemonade to three construction workers, who were standing in line. Two ladies coming out of the post office stood behind them to buy lemonade from "that cute little boy."

Max and Gordy exchanged angry glances. This was definitely not fair. Making a million dollars was Max's idea. Not Austin's.

"Hi, guys," Austin called when his customers left. "Want a drink?"

"We're not thirsty," said Max. He could still taste the warm lemonade, which was starting to rise up to his throat. He probably wouldn't touch the stuff for the rest of the summer.

"How's business?" asked Max. He knew the answer even before Austin gave it.

"It's great. I figured I'd get some practice on my own before I'm old enough to join up with you." He poured himself a cup of water and drank it down.

"What's the matter, Austin?" asked Gordy. "Don't you trust your lemonade?"

"I don't want to drink up all my profits," Austin answered. "When I'm thirsty, I drink the water. And I sell the lemonade."

Max watched the people walking in and out of the post office. He watched the construction workers wiping sweat off their faces. So many people. So many *thirsty* people. Why hadn't he thought to come here?

"You picked a pretty good spot to set up your stand," said Max. He hated to admit it, but it was true.

"Yeah," said Austin. "I knew these men would be here today. I knew they'd be thirsty. You just have to be in the right place at the right time. You've got to know your market. Know your customers. Too bad they won't be here tomorrow. I'll have to figure out something else to do."

Max watched Austin empty the cup of money into his pockets. He could see the quarters, nickels, and dimes pouring out of the cup. He even saw a dollar bill.

"Boy. Making a million dollars sure is fun," said Austin. "I can't wait until tomorrow."

The Boy Who Invented TV

The Story of Philo Farnsworth

by
Kathleen Krull

illustrated by
Greg Couch

No sooner did Philo Farnsworth learn to talk than he asked a question. Then another, and another. His parents answered as best they could.

Noticing Philo's interest in anything mechanical, his father took the three-year-old boy to see a train at a station. At first Philo was afraid this huge, noisy thing might be a monster. But the nice engineer invited the boy up into the cab with him, explaining a bit about how steam-powered trains worked.

That night Philo sat at the kitchen table and drew detailed pictures of what went on inside the motor of a train.

Two new machines captivated Philo as he grew up. One was a hand-cranked telephone, purchased by a neighbor. Holding the phone one day, hearing the voice of his beloved aunt, six-year-old Philo got goose bumps. After all, she lived a long ways away!

Another neighbor brought a hand-cranked phonograph to a dance. Music swirling out of a machine—it was almost impossible to believe.

"These things seemed like magic to me," Philo said later. Besides being incredibly clever, the inventions brought people together in whole new ways.

Philo's father shared his wonder. On clear summer nights, as they lay in the grass and gazed at the stars, his father told him about Alexander Graham Bell and the telephone, Thomas Edison and the phonograph. Inventors—these became Philo's heroes.

Away on a temporary job, his father appointed Philo, the oldest of five children, the "man" in the family. Philo was eight. His many chores included feeding the pigs, milking and grazing the cow, fetching wood for the stove. He did get his own pony—Tippy.

It was also a sort of reward to skip school for a while. Bullies there teased him about his unusual name. Shy and serious, Philo didn't fight back.

He found it far more appealing to practice reading with his grandmother's Sears, Roebuck catalog. It had toys … as well as cameras, alarm clocks, and machines that used a new, invisible source of power. Electricity, it was called.

Electrical Devices

In his spare time, Philo raised lambs and sold them. When he had enough money saved up, he visited his grandmother to pick a bicycle out of her catalog.

But somehow, she talked him into ordering a violin instead. Philo did love the sound of music, its orderly rhythms. And even at age ten, he dreamed of fame. Maybe he could find it by creating music like what he heard on the neighbor's phonograph.

Soon he was performing in dance bands, making five dollars every Friday night.

Playing the violin was one more thing for the bullies to tease him about. Then one day Philo fought back, and the teasing ended.

Trying for a better life, the Farnsworths moved from Utah to an Idaho farm with fields of beets and potatoes. Eleven-year-old Philo drove one of their covered wagons, carrying a crate of piglets, a cage of hens, his violin, and their new prize possession—a phonograph.

Arriving in the Snake River Valley, he noticed something up in the air—power lines. Their new home was wired for electricity! A generator ran the lights and water heater, the hay stacker and grain elevator, and other farm equipment.

And up in the attic was another welcome surprise. A shelf of old popular-science magazines, with thrilling articles about magnetism, electricity, and those new "magic boxes"—radios. Philo promptly claimed this as his bedroom. His chores began before dawn, but he trained himself to wake up an hour early so he could switch on the light and read in bed. Any spare money he had went to buy more magazines.

That's when he saw the word "television" for the first time. It meant a machine that was something like a radio, only it sent pictures instead of sounds.

It didn't actually exist yet, but scientists were racing to invent one.

The electric generator broke down a lot, and repairs were costly. Each time the repairman came, Philo bombarded him with questions.

After yet another breakdown, Philo set out to fix the machine himself. He took it apart, cleaned it, put it back together, and pressed the "on" button. It worked.

Philo's father was enormously proud of him. From then on, he was the Farnsworths' electrical engineer.

Philo tinkered with broken motors, reels of wire, old tools. He devised gadgets to hook up to the generator—anything to make his chores easier, like installing lights in the barn.

His least favorite thing was washing clothes—hours of standing while pushing and pulling the lever that swished the water around the washtub. So he attached a motor with pulleys to the lever to make it churn on its own, leaving him extra time to read.

When he was thirteen, Philo entered a contest sponsored by *Science and Invention* magazine. Using what he'd learned about magnets, he pictured an ignition lock that would make the new Model T Fords harder to steal.

When he won the contest, Philo spent the prize money on his first pair of proper long pants. Wearing boyish short pants at the Friday dances was just plain embarrassing.

Philo went on investigating television. An article called "Pictures that Fly Through the Air" stimulated him. Scientists were having no luck—so far their ideas resulted in crude mechanical devices that used whirling disks and mirrors.

Philo doubted any disk could whirl fast enough to work. Much better to do the job electronically. To harness electrons, those mysterious, invisible particles that traveled at the speed of light . . .

Pictures that Fly Through the Air

Photocell *Amplifier* *Radio Transmitter* *Radio Receiver* *Mask*

Mask *Neon Tube(?)*

Televised Subject *Scanning Disk* *Motor 1200 r.p.m.(?)* *Reproducing Disk* *You, Looking in*

To Generator *B. The Receiver*

A. The Transmitter

...practical application ...new ways of splitting ...pictures into electrons

Though it may seem far-fetched, scientis... trying for years...

107

One bright, sunny day, fourteen-year-old Philo plowed the potato fields. It was the best chore for thinking—out in the open country by himself. Back and forth, back and forth . . . the plow created rows of overturned earth. He looked behind him at the lines he was carving—perfectly parallel.

Then he almost fell off the plow seat. All his thoughts fused together. Instead of seeing rows of dirt, he saw a way to create television: breaking down images into parallel lines of light, capturing them and transmitting them as electrons, then reassembling them for a viewer. If it was done quickly enough, people's eyes could be tricked into seeing a complete picture instead of lines. "Capturing light in a bottle" was how he thought of it—using electricity, not a machine with moving parts inside.

Philo's grin was wide. He told the idea to his father, who tried to understand but couldn't keep up with his son.

In the autumn Philo started high school, riding horseback four miles each way.

Mr. Tolman, the senior chemistry teacher, noticed that this freshman devoured books the way other students ate popcorn. He started tutoring Philo, coming in early and leaving late.

One day Mr. Tolman passed by a study hall and heard loud talking. Philo's latest hero was Albert Einstein, with his controversial new theory of relativity. Now Philo stood at the front of the room, enthusiastically explaining it to his classmates, step by step.

Usually Philo spoke little, with a halting voice. But when he could share his knowledge of science, he was a different boy.

Philo had been aching to discuss the idea he'd gotten in the potato field with someone who might understand. One day he finally told Mr. Tolman. All over the blackboard, he drew diagrams of his television.

His teacher was boggled. Philo ripped a page out of the notebook he always kept in his shirt pocket. He scribbled a diagram of an all-electric camera, the kind of converter he envisioned. An Image Dissector, he called it.

Mr. Tolman pointed out that it would take a lot of money to build such a thing. The only way he could think of helping was to encourage Philo to go on to college.

But Philo was forced to quit college at eighteen, after his father died. By then the family had moved back to Utah, to the town of Provo, and Philo supported them by working at all sorts of jobs in nearby Salt Lake City.

His favorite one was repairing radios. Though commercial radio broadcasts had started four years earlier, Philo couldn't believe, in 1924, how many people still hadn't heard one. On weekends he organized "radio parties" so his friends could gather around one of the bulky wooden cabinets and listen to the new stations.

Pem Gardner, the girl next door, was interested in radio—and also in Philo.

Wasn't it funny, Philo remarked to Pem, how they liked to watch the radio even though there was nothing to see? Radio was such a fine way to bring folks together. And television, he sensed, would be even better.

Thanks to his obsession with television, Philo had already lost one girlfriend, who called him too much of a dreamer. But Pem cheered him on. Now what he needed was money. He grew a mustache to look older, bought a new blue suit, and started to call himself Phil.

He met two California businessmen, and over dinner one night, he took them through a step-by-step explanation of his Image Dissector: a camera tube that would dissect an image into a stream of electrons, converting them into pulses of electrical current. A receiver would capture the current, then convert it back into points of light—the original image.

As he talked, he got more and more passionate. After scanning images line by line, just like rows in a potato field, this machine would beam them into homes. That was the best thing about television, he said—it would let families and whole communities share the same stories. By making people less ignorant of one another, he went on, it would teach and inspire. Maybe even lead to world peace.

The two businessmen exchanged looks, then agreed to put up $6,000 so Philo could build the first model. They gave him a year to make it work.

Philo hit upon a way to work twenty-four hours a day: he set himself problems to solve while sleeping.

He filed for several government patents that would protect his ideas for the next seventeen years. It was important to him to keep control, to get credit.

On their wedding night, he turned to Pem. "I have to tell you, there is another woman in my life—and her name is Television."

Pem helped out. Their first lab was their dining room table in Hollywood. Pem learned to use a precision welder to make tube elements—everything had to be built from scratch. When they needed a break, they went to one of the new talking movies.

Finally they got the lights, wires, and tubes to work in unison. But at the first demonstration, Philo forgot one item. He failed to take the power surge into account. The entire Image Dissector exploded. Pem, who took notes about everything, labeled this experiment "Bang! Pop! Sizzle!"

Still, Philo was able to find new investors, who gave him another year.

117

At his new lab in San Francisco, Philo met the deadline. In 1927,
a small group of people watched as the first image in history flickered
on a TV.

He said, "That's it, folks. We've done it—there you have electronic
television."

That first image was not fancy. It was a straight line,
blurry and bluish. Later he was able to show a dollar sign,
and then the motion of cigarette smoke.

The first person to be televised was his true love, Pem,
who didn't know she was on camera and had her eyes closed.

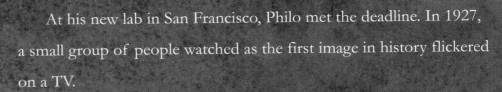

The following year, in front of a crowd of reporters, twenty-two-year-old Philo Farnsworth announced the invention of television.

That night he was behind the wheel of a borrowed car. He and Pem were heading home after catching a movie with another couple. They stopped to buy the *San Francisco Chronicle* from a newsboy. And there was a photo of Philo holding his invention. The article praised a "young genius" for creating a "revolutionary light machine."

Pem and his friends read it aloud, bouncing up and down, yelling. Philo was silent, but a big smile crossed his face.

He was a real inventor, like his heroes—someone who connected people, a shaper of the world to come. Thanks to him, the future would include **TV.**

Lunch Money

by Carol Diggory Shields

Don't ask Dad—he never has any.
Grandma's purse has a nickel and a penny,
Mom has a five, but the car needs gas.
Here's a dirty quarter someone found in the grass.
Checked all our pockets—nothing but gum.
Piggy bank, piggy bank, here I come!

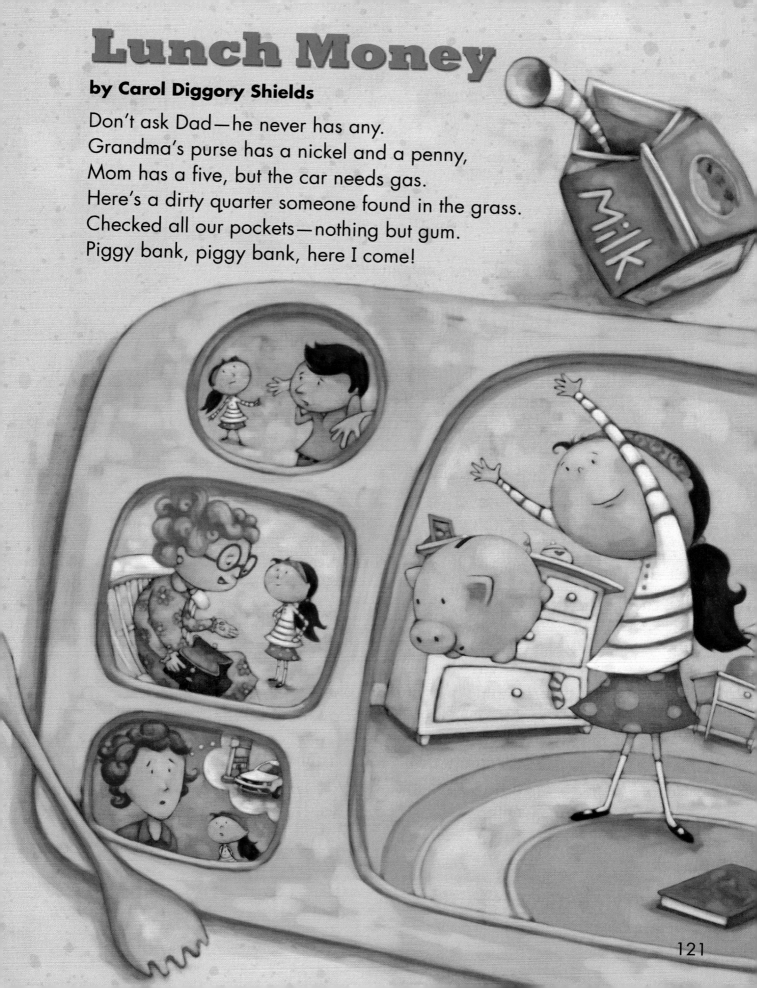

Gold

by Pat Mora
illustrated by Thomas Locker

When Sun paints the desert
with its gold,
I climb the hills.
Wind runs round boulders, ruffles
my hair. I sit on my favorite rock,
lizards for company, a rabbit,
ears stiff in the shade
of a saguaro.
In the wind, we're all
eye to eye.

Sparrow on saguaro watches
rabbit watch us in the gold
of sun setting.
Hawk sails on waves of light, sees
sparrow, rabbit, lizards, me,
our eyes shining,
watching red and purple
      sand rivers stream down the hills.

I stretch my arms wide as the sky
like hawk extends her wings
in all the gold light of this, home.

Bronze Cowboys

by Carole Boston Weatherford

When bison roamed the wild, wild West
dark riders rode the Pony Express
over the mountains, across the plains,
past coyotes, bobcats and wagon trains.
Bronze cowboys rode in cattle drives
where deserts met the turquoise skies.
They busted broncos and bulldogged steer,
made peace with the Indians and showed no fear.
A mail carrier named Stagecoach Mary
fought off wolves on the lonesome prairie.
Nat Love was the surest shot in the land.
Bill Pickett was known as a mean cowhand.
Around the campfire, they strummed guitars,
imagined they could lasso stars.

Homework  by Russell Hoban

Homework sits on top of Sunday, squashing Sunday flat.
Homework has the smell of Monday, homework's very fat.
Heavy books and piles of paper, answers I don't know.
Sunday evening's almost finished, now I'm going to go
Do my homework in the kitchen. Maybe just a snack,
Then I'll sit right down and start as soon as I run back
For some chocolate sandwich cookies. Then I'll really do
All that homework in a minute. First I'll see what new
Show they've got on television in the living room.
Everybody's laughing there, but misery and gloom
And a full refrigerator are where I am at.
I'll just have another sandwich. Homework's very fat.

A Last Word About Inventions

By Charise Mericle Harper

Some inventions solve a problem,
   like glasses to help you see.
Then there are others just for fun,
   like skates or the Frisbee.

Inventions can be lucky,
   like the great potato chip,
or even come from other lands,
   like doughnuts on a ship.

Inventors can be young
   or as old as ninety-three,
they just need imagination
   to see things creatively.

SMART

by Shel Silverstein

My dad gave me one dollar bill
'Cause I'm his smartest son,
And I swapped it for two shiny quarters
'Cause two is more than one!

And then I took the quarters
And traded them to Lou
For three dimes—I guess he don't know
That three is more than two!

Just then, along came old blind Bates
And just 'cause he can't see
He gave me four nickels for my three dimes,
And four is more than three!

And I took the nickels to Hiram Coombs
Down at the seed-feed store,
And the fool gave me five pennies for them,
And five is more than four!

And then I went and showed my dad,
And he got red in the cheeks
And closed his eyes and shook his head—
Too proud of me to speak!

"Smart" from *Where the Sidewalk Ends* by Shel Silverstein. Copyright © 1974, renewed 202 Evil Eye Music, LLC. Reprinted with permission from the Estate of Shel Silverstein and HarperCollins Children's Books.

Illustrations

25-29 Marcos Calo

31-36 Paul Hoffman

121 Kristin Varner

124 Dan Andreasen

125 James Bernadin

Photographs

Photo locators denoted as follows: Top (T), Center (C), Bottom (B), Left (L), Right (R), Background (Bkgd)

36 Chris Wilson/Alamy; **55** Michael Pitts/naturepl; **56** Science Source.